# MATTERS OF GREAT INDIFFERENCE

*Reflections on modern rural living*

## — *VOLUME 2* —

GW00992107

# MATTERS OF GREAT INDIFFERENCE

*Reflections on modern rural living*

— *VOLUME 2* —

## Jim O'Brien

LIMERICK WRITERS' CENTRE
PUBLISHING

First published in Ireland by

The Limerick Writers' Centre
c/o The Umbrella Project
78 O'Connell Street, Limerick, Ireland

www.limerickwriterscentre.com
www.facebook.com/limerickwriterscentre

1 3 5 7 9 10 8 6 4 2

Book Design: Lotte Bender
Cover Image: Jim O'Brien
Cover Design and Artwork: Detail Factory, Limerick

Managing Editor LWC: Dominic Taylor

ISBN 978-1-7392070-0-7

Print copy available: www.limerickwriterscentre.com
Also available as an e-book

A CIP catalogue number for this publication is available from The British Library

*Dedication*
For my parents, Miceál and Eily, and my sisters and
brothers, Olive, Tony, Marie, Ger, Denis, Pat, Eithne,
Declan, Elaine and Anne

# Contents

# Preface

This is the second volume of *Matters of Great Indifference* and includes a selection of columns that appeared in the *Farming Independent* between October 2020 to October 2022.

I have been writing a column on rural living for the *Farming Independent* since 2017 and writing for the property section of the paper since 2010. While the last collection was inspired in part by my travels around the country, I have been confined to barracks by Covid and other considerations since then and perhaps this work is more reflective and more the product of a semi-monastic existence.

My reflection is fed by observation and reminiscence; observation of the life I'm living and the context in which I am living it. It is also fed by the lives I have lived from my childhood in Kildimo, Co Limerick to my formative years in Carmelite College in Castlemartyr, Co Cork and my time in Maynooth. The places I have called and call home in Foynes, Co Limerick, Rosenallis, Co Laois and O'Gonnelloe in Co Clare are deep wells I draw from, as are the plethora of careers I've taken on as I try to discover what I want to be when I grow up.

In the main, the pieces are presented chronologically and reflect the things that have had an impact on my life and the world around me over the last two years. The big and the small are included, from the Covid pandemic to the war in Ukraine, the arrival of a new pup and the departure of my children.

As you will see, the climate catastrophe and our pulverisation of the planet preoccupies me, it is the issue of our time, time that is fast running out.

Don't worry, I do find lots to smile and laugh about. I hope you find something between these covers that will comfort, challenge, amuse and touch you.

The title comes from my grandfather who went to the pub most nights to drink a few pints, play a game of cards and discuss what he called 'matters of great indifference'.

O'Gonnelloe
October 2022

# 1

# When our tractors were Porsches

Growing up in Co Limerick the seasons of the year were marked by the arrival and departure of visitors. These included the swallow, wild geese and human beings. Americans generally came in the summer, exiles based in England came in February during what they called 'half term', and Dubliners dropped in on their way to the beaches of Kerry or coming back from the Willie Clancy festival.

I remember one particular visitor, a German named Paul, who came once a year to service our tractor. Believe it or not, we had a series of Porsche tractors, isn't that posh? In fact, it borders on the onomatopoeic. Like its motor car cousin, the Volkswagen Beetle, the Porsche tractor had an air-cooled engine with a distinctive tukka-tukka-tukka sound.

It was quite different from the more common Massey and Ford machines and required some specialist care. This became a problem after the company stopped making tractors in 1964, so, mechanics like Paul were dispatched around the world servicing, repairing and supplying parts for the Porsches that remained in service.

He would arrive in our backyard in a Volkswagen campervan that doubled as a mobile workshop. The front and middle of the vehicle contained his living quarters, including a couch-bed, cooker and storage. The back door opened to reveal an array of tools and parts, all neatly stored in wooden compartments where, in true Teutonic order, everything had a place and everything was in its place. As children we didn't have to be told to stay away from that section of the van, one look at it would tell you that a child would wreak untold destruction were he or she to be let loose anywhere near it.

To us, Paul was an exotic creature, a welcome injection of variety into a monocultural and almost self-contained rural world. From what I can remember, he was completely bald, wore rimless spectacles and looked more like a professor than a mechanic. My father had complete confidence in him, treating him like a demi-god or an oracle 'who knew what he was doing', an accolade reserved for a certain few. For weeks afterwards he would sing the praises of Paul repeating over and over, "This tractor is going like a clock, you can't beat the Germans."

When I progressed to secondary school and made 'townie' friends they wouldn't believe me when I told them we owned a Porsche tractor. As there were no mobile phones at that time, and very few people possessed a camera, I couldn't organise a photograph to prove my story. Indeed, for a short period of time we had two Porsches, a Standard and a Super. My father had up-graded to the Super model and was waiting to have the front-loader transferred from the humble Standard before parting with it. In the meantime, my aunt and uncle lost a haybarn full of hay to fire and the little Standard, with its loader, was pressed into service and spent a week loading mountains of hay gathered by the neighbours to replace what was lost. I remember my father saying it did the work of a thousand men.

If bumper stickers had been in fashion at that time, we would have had one attached to the family saloon that read, 'Never mind this, my tractor is a Porsche.' As the 1960s gave way to the 1970s Paul stopped coming and we moved on from the trusty Porsche.

I digress, I was getting around to telling you about another annual visitor to our house; a man who would arrive in August, just before my parents went for their holidays to Liscannor. He would suggest that they might use the holiday to take up golf and play a few rounds at nearby Lahinch. My father would tell him the only rounds he was interested in were the ones he would buy over the counter in Joe McHugh's pub. As the years moved on, and the children in the house progressed into young adulthood, our August visitor would wonder if any of us had even the slightest sign of marital intentions, "Come on," he would say, "I'm blue mowldy for a day out."

It is only now, after all these weeks of confinement, I know what he meant. The anxiety for a day out is rising in me and I can almost feel the blue 'mowld' gathering around my itchy feet. The absence of visitors and the limited nature of social interaction is causing the unventilated mind to fall in on itself.

Meanwhile, Christmas is coming and the Scrooge-like pronouncements emanating from Leinster House are far from encouraging, there's more 'ho-ho-ho' to be found in a 1980s budget speech. We can only hope that visitors will soon be free to come and go as they please, until then we can only remember a time when they did, a golden era, when even our tractors were Porsches.

# 2

# What lies beyond the mortal ditch?

It is November, a month when we traditionally remember our dead. Those of us seasoned by length of days find that, with every year, our remembering more and more, puts us in touch with the reality of our own mortality.

What happens when the great silence falls has forever exercised minds, hearts and imaginations. It's ironic, but on the flip side of the absolute certainty of death there is complete uncertainty, an eternal question mark. Philosophies of life and faith systems have been built on attempts at answering this question. Armies have gone to war believing their answer and their connections in eternity would give them victory, if not on the battlefield, in the hereafter where their faith and courage would be rewarded. There is a transactional element to the notion of the beyond that colours many belief systems.

In our religious culture, the prospect of eternal reward was a key motivating factor in living the good life and remaining faithful to one's religious practice and values. In that belief system, life at this side of the abyss is but 'a vale of tears', where existence is a thing to be endured before we enter the land of milk and honey at the other side of the cosmic Jordan.

The hardness of life and the suffering it entails, is nothing compared to the glories of eternity.

Belief in eternal happiness and fulfilment is undoubtedly a source of deep comfort. It can offer meaning to lives that would otherwise be ground down by the absurdity of it all.

Conjectures about what happens after we breathe our last vary widely. Here in the west our understanding follows the Greek model where, once you cross the River Styx into the realm of Hades, your eternity depends on how you behaved yourself in life. In the Greek understanding, the virtuous and heroic could forever enjoy the Elysian Fields in the Isles of the Blessed, while those who lived a blameless, but relatively harmless life could pass a pleasant eternity in the Meadows of Asphodel.

However, those whose lives were wicked would be sent to the Fields of Punishment where the treatment befitted one's misdemeanours. The less severe cases were deprived of consciousness while the most severe cases had to endure particular torments. Poor Sisyphus, for example, spent eternity rolling a boulder up a hill only to see it roll back down again every time he reached the summit.

The Christian notion of eternity, of heaven and hell, have similar themes of reward and punishment, where your eternity will mirror the choices you made in life. I remember a number of years ago driving with an old friend who declared himself to be less than impressed by my fondness for the accelerator. "What are you afraid of?" I asked, "aren't you well prepared to meet your maker?"

"Given the life I've led," he responded, "I'm afraid it's the bucko with the horns I'll be facing."

All belief systems don't have such stark transactional alternatives in their notion of what it's like at the other side of the great divide. Many have reincarnation as an article of faith providing a few opportunities to prove yourself. It's a bit like the backdoor system in the GAA championships. The Greeks had elements of this, and many eastern religions believe life is a series of incarnations where you can elevate yourself to a higher level of being each time you come back.

If I am to be reincarnated, I want to be tall and thin the next time around, knowing my luck I'll probably come back as a giraffe.

The question as to what becomes of us when our breath takes leave of our bodies continues to be a mystery, one that many deal with in the context of a deeply held faith. Others hold that eternity is now, that 'this' is as good as it gets, or as good as you make it.

Not too many of us spend our days contemplating the ultimate questions. Even those in the vortex of bereavement may not spend too much time with the mystery, but remain consumed by the loss, the absence and the finality. However, the mystery is always around us. Our books, songs, stories, hymns, films, jokes, plays, paintings, sculptures, scriptures, fears and phobias are laced with traces of death and probes into the beyond.

Contemplating the mystery, I try to avoid getting lost in the detail of what it is or isn't like and try to avoid reducing it to a transaction.

There is a broad sweep to the story of the universe, and when faced with the enormity of it I tend to fall back on a few bits of confidence and consolation. There are three in particular; developments in modern physics, a piece of Buddhist wisdom and the words of a Christian mediaeval mystic.

A school of physics in the Einstein line holds that we are essentially energy and energy doesn't die, it goes on and on. This chimes with a primary tenet of Buddhist wisdom which tells us "Nothing is lost in the universe". Finally, the words of Julian of Norwich assure us, that "all will be well, and all manner of things will be well."

# 3

# Speeding through America

I'm inclined to think there was a lot of male regression last week as the marathon US election count dragged on interminably. Simple domestic tasks, which the modern male had only recently been trained to accomplish, were once again remaining undone. The toilet seat was standing in the upright position like a monument to male oblivion. Dirty dishes were heaped in unwashed mounds on the coffee table, on the worktop and the draining board. Clothes that should have been retrieved from the washing line were flapping in the wind like giant, wet, Floridian hanging chads. The male political junkie becomes almost feral when elections come around.

Last week, I was that soldier, lost between phone, computer and TV screen, wandering around unshaven, unkempt and distracted. I even had the gall to wonder aloud how come so many Americans had voted for the most misogynistic president of all time. The current consort said nothing, realising that, as well as not doing the ironing, I don't even do irony.

Aside from the near collapse in gender equality in the home, the US election was an amazing spectacle. It was also a great lesson in the geography of the United States. By the time it was over we were all experts on the demographics of Arizona's Maricopa County and the racial makeup of counties Erie and Monroe in Pennsylvania.

I was sitting on the couch late into the night during the marathon election, watching the news from Georgia. The current consort had retired after concluding there would be no further developments until later in the morning, it being 2.30am. I was given a list of things to be done before I too retired. I had doors to lock, a dishwasher to kick-start and devices to switch off.

I was half listening to CNN's John King going through the counties around Atlanta until he mentioned Cobb County, the very utterance of which, caused me to freeze. I have reason to remember Cobb, its name is stitched into my psyche since December 23, 1995.

I was driving from Chicago to Florida with my aunt and a mutual friend to spend Christmas in the sunshine state. On the beltway around the Georgian capital, I hadn't noticed the speed limit had dropped from 65mph to 55mph.

Unfortunately for me, a policeman parked in the highway median noticed that I hadn't noticed. With lights flashing and siren blaring, he 'pulled me over.'

I was searching my wallet for my driving license when the lawman appeared at the driver's door. He asked me to step out of the 'cawr' and explain why I was speeding. We had a mannerly difference of opinion about the speed I was doing, but when he heard my accent and saw my license he said, "I have no choice but to arrest you, sir, you are from out of town and unlikely to appear at court to pay your fine."

At this point may aunt alighted from the car and proceeded to berate the officer for his treatment of 'this young man, a visitor to our country'. The policeman was impervious to her indignation, and I suggested to her that she might be making matters worse for me.

"I am arresting this man and, Mam, you can follow us in your car."

"Where are you taking him?" she asked.

"I'm taking him to the nearest place where I can process this offence, there's a women's correctional facility just a few blocks away."

"You're taking him to jail. To a women's jail?"

"Auntie, leave him alone," I asked, "I'll be fine."

It was December 23, the night before Christmas Eve, and here I was in the back of a cop car in Atlanta, Georgia, heading for a women's prison. I hoped Santa would be able to find me.

At the prison the officers in the reception booth didn't know what to do with me. The policeman told them that as prison officers they were also court officials and could process traffic offenses. After much phone calling to various bodies across Atlanta and much talk about what they were doing for Christmas they eventually dealt with the charge. I paid a fine of $51 to get me out of jail. I still have the receipt identifying Cobb County as the location of my offence.

Once I'd paid up, the policeman said, "You are free to go now, sir."

"Excuse me," the woman behind the counter said, "he is our prisoner, and we have the authority to release him."

"No, he is my prisoner," the policeman protested. They fought over me for about ten minutes before I was eventually released. Outside the jail by my aunt proceeded to give the arresting officer another dressing down.

"Come on Auntie," I said, let's get out of here."

That's the last time I was in Cobb County. I felt some touch of redemption in the wee hours of Friday morning when CNN announced that the citizens in the place of my detention were set to give Biden the nod. All is forgiven.

Now, if you will excuse me, I have a bit of ironing to attend to.

# 4

# The Great Hunger and the great silence

Over two Monday nights I watched that excellent two-part television programme, *The Hunger: The Story of the Irish Famine*. Broadcast on RTE and written by Ruán Magan it was a powerful piece of work. There was an immediacy to its portrayal of the awfulness and horror of what happened to ordinary people. Equally immediate was its depiction of the cynicism, racism and heartless opportunism exhibited by many of those at the upper echelons of government, and to our shame, by neighbours and local officials.

Watching it I felt a rising sense of dismay at what was unfolding and a rumbling anger at the myriad of injustices and tone deafness that exacerbated the tragedy.

The economic and social unsustainability of the situation prevailing immediately prior to the arrival of the blight is plain to see; a burgeoning population very much dependent on a single food source, the potato.

Aside from some successes on the part of Robert Peel's Tory government, from 1846 the policies pursued by John Lord Russell's Whig government deepened the misery and increased the death toll. What happened will forever stand as an indictment of him and his administration.

The figures speak for themselves, before the Famine the population of the island of Ireland stood at 8m people. Ireland is the only country in Europe to have a population lower than it had in 1840, we have never recovered.

Like any great event of historical significance, the Famine can become so huge and so iconic that we lose the sense of its reality. Ruán Magan's programme broke through the iconography and the epic nature of the event to bring us face-to-face with real people, people with names like ours, people who walked, worked and died in the places that we call home. We are but a remove from their ghosts.

By coincidence, my attention was recently drawn to a paper delivered in 1995 by the late Mainchín Seoighe, a Limerickman, renowned local historian and writer. The short paper, like Magan's TV programme, combines statistic and anecdote to paint a graphic picture of the reality of the Famine in Co Limerick.

To my total surprise my own home parish is singled out as one of the most severely affected. In examining the townland population losses throughout the county between 1841 and 1851 Seoighe notes that townlands in my home place had population losses of 85pc, 81pc, 70pc, 68pc, 60pc and 50pc.

I grew up totally unaware of this, my grandparents never spoke about it. The Famine was something I studied in the history books. It was about as real to me as the Battle of Waterloo, and yet, the inhabitants of entire townlands in the place where I grew up disappeared in the 1840s and no-one mentioned it. I knew more about the Cromwellian and Williamite sieges of Limerick that predated it by 200 and 150 years than I knew about the local impact of the Famine.

Local history groups do excellent work recording the history of the locality. Members of one in my own locality are specifically acknowledged by Mainchin Seoighe for their contribution to his article on the Famine. But what is preventing us from owning this knowledge? Why do I know the name of Cromwell's son-in-law who took over the command of his forces at Limerick? Why do I know the name of the Dutch general who commanded the Williamite artillery at Limerick. Why do I know the name of the French general who had his head shot off at the Battle of Aughrim? Why do I know all this and yet I don't know the name of one person who died of hunger or disease in my home place, one of the worst affected in the country?

Is it survivor guilt? Was the Great Hunger followed by a great silence? Perhaps it is more than coincidence that the language spoken by the majority of the people in Ireland in the 19th century, like the population size, never recovered from the Famine. Is it taking it too far to say that the Irish language was critically wounded in the calamity but was finished off by the great silence that followed? Perhaps we chose to forget the very sounds, the very echo of the only words that could possibly hold and express the awfulness of what had occurred.

In these days, when the place of history in our schools' curriculum is under threat, it is even more important that we remember and learn. It is vital that we remember and learn the local stories, the names of our neighbours who lie under the local sod or fled the pestilence.

Why should we remember? Because it is our holocaust.

I'll leave the last word to Mainchín Seoighe, "Surely, we, the descendants of the survivors, should ensure, as far as lies in our power, that no other people anywhere in the world shall ever experience the like again."

# 5

# Fragility and ingenuity come face-to-face

There was a beautiful yellow flower growing in the lawn during the summer. It bloomed in the morning but disappeared every afternoon at about four, pulling its petals into the nucleus around which they were anchored. In its evening camouflage of green it hid in the grass until the sun tempted it to show itself again, glorious in its bright, yellow daywear.

As the winter settles into its depth and our crescent of the planet sinks to the nadir of its long sleep, we too return to our nucleus. For a few short days we fold ourselves into that small pod of our kin, until the year turns, and we shake ourselves into another January.

For many, there will be no novelty in this turning to the hearth, most of us have been confined to the orbit of our inner circle for months; the only difference will be the tinsel and turkey.

What I will miss this year are the communal bits, the gatherings, the sounds of the carols and the echoes of the perennial Christmas hits, sweetly sung or belted out in their respective beauty and raucousness. I will miss squeezing through packed pubs to meet friends, I will miss the spontaneous hugs on the street from those who are home for the few days and in town to get the last bits.

I will miss wandering from house to house. 'Dropping in' will not happen, only arranged encounters organised with the precision of a state visit by a delicate monarch with an allergy to everything.

The airports and ferry terminals wont echo with the whoops of joy as exit doors slide open and overloaded trolleys are abandoned by returnees who run like wild things to throw their arms around those who stayed at home.

There will be many an absence, absences that won't be compensated for by Zoom, Skype, phone or facetime. There is no virtual replacement for the satin touch of the skin, the sight and feel of the face globed in your hands. Nothing in cyber can imitate the intimacy of that last nocturnal peep you take at the slumbering, curly heads sleeping deep on pillows that smell of home.

When we look back at the broad sweep of this epic year we will realise it was the communal bits that saved us. These communal efforts of our state, our public servants, our volunteers, our private companies, and most of all, the quiet courage of those who, day after day, returned to the hospitals and care homes bringing an armoury of skills and the balm of humanity as they faced the unimaginable.

It is the communal bits that kept it together for us, and it is a communal bit, a historic sharing of knowledge and information, that brought us vaccines, manufactured miracles of human ingenuity that will enable us to turn and move on.

The year 2020 will forever carry the label, 'a year like no other'. When they replay the old newsclips and reel in this year, no doubt the yellow and black signs urging us to stay apart, the sight of people wearing masks and the sombre pictures of coffins on army trucks will be employed to tell the tale.

Many stories will be told of profound and redeeming acts of human kindness, of simple things that made an extraordinary difference; neighbours shopping for one another, friends visiting at a distance to make sure everything is alright and strangers holding the hands of strangers, easing them along the last stretch into the beyond.

As Christmas 2020 arrives, the tidings from laboratories across the planet are tidings of comfort and joy that merit a global chorus of 'Hallelujah'. In this year like no other our fragility and ingenuity came face-to-face, and while we have reason to hope that our ingenuity will have the upper hand, the stark reminders of our fragility should temper any arrogance.

There is a tangible and understandable nervousness as we face 2021, things have changed, but how deep and enduring the change remains to be seen. I am reminded of TS Eliot's poem, 'The Journey of the Magi' where he imagines the impact the visit to Bethlehem had on the triumvirate of wise men,

"We returned to our places, these Kingdoms,
But no longer at ease here, in the old dispensation,
With an alien people clutching their gods."

# 6

# Harbour the intention and its time will come

It is only the tick of a clock, a blip on a digital screen, the twitch of a second hand that takes us from one year to the next. Every twelve months we give enormous significance to that fleeting moment ascribing to it the power to define ends and beginnings. There is a sort of cultural pressure to mark the moment with a significant change in one's life, one's behaviour or one's attitudes.

Even those of us whose appetite for resolutions has been well shorn of its edge are tempted to turn yet another new leaf as December 31 transmogrifies into January 1. Decades of failed attempts at instituting even the most minor of changes don't prevent us from setting more deadlines and trying again.

I was a smoker once, and despite many gallant New Year attempts to 'rise out of' the habit I eventually quit in an unplanned, drama-free manner. It happened without warning on an unremarkable day in March 1997. The previous night I attended a social gathering of old friends in Limerick where we talked, tippled and smoked our way into the small hours.

The following morning, feeling somewhat the worse for wear, I gathered my belongings and prepared to return to work in Galway. In a final sweep of the flat to ensure I had everything I picked up my pack of cigarettes. I looked inside to see how many I had left and knew if I put the pack in my pocket, I would have one smoked before I got to Ennis. For some reason, I decided to leave them after me. I never again bought a pack of cigarettes and, while I took the odd cigar, I never really smoked again.

There was nothing significant about the date and time I chose to leave my nicotine addiction behind, it just happened on a damp morning in March.

Something similar happened in relation to taking exercise. As regular readers of this column will know I am not the sporty type, so it came as a surprise to myself when, out of the blue, I took up walking for exercise. At that time, about 18 years ago, I was working in Dublin and commuting from Laois every day, spending between three and four hours in the car. If I chose to climb the stairs to the office it was the only exercise I got, more often than not I took the lift. I was well aware that my lifestyle was very unhealthy, the weight was piling on but I avoided doing anything about it.

On a Wednesday morning in spring 2002 I woke early and remembered it was Ash Wednesday. As I lay there it struck me that I no longer marked the Lenten season, so I decided to get up and go for a half an hour walk before doing the morning chores and setting out for work.

As soon as the children were old enough to be left in the house unsupervised, the current consort joined me on the morning preambulation. Aside from occasional outbreaks of laziness, we have been pounding the roads since. Indeed, during the lockdown we doubled the daily dosage. We now walk for an hour a day and are in danger of becoming imbued with the self-satisfaction of the lycra-clad cyclists that whizz past us like spindly Martians.

Instituting changes to improve one's life is not confined by time and space. This preoccupation with bingeing on reform in the early and bleak days of January is a recipe for disappointment. I remember two years ago, in the first column of the year, I admitted to having three part-written books sitting in my writing folder. I publicly promised I would have one of them done and dusted by the end of the year.

As usual, I overshot the landing area. Last October, a year later than promised, I eventually finished and published a book. Even then, I cheated a little; the tome that made it to the shelves is a compilation of these weekly columns and not one of the three unfinished works mentioned previously. Aside from some occasional tampering, the manuscripts are still sitting in their folders, untended to and unloved, awaiting completion or deletion. However, the intention is there, and its time will come.

We beat ourselves up over New Year's resolutions, Lenten promises and bucket lists, but it is important to realise there is no one up there in the heavens with a stopwatch timing and measuring what we do with our lives. The sky is not going to fall in if all our good intentions are not realised within a certain timeframe.

I think it is far better to harbour the intention and its time will come.

# 7

# Bring us to April and its bright promise

There is no such thing as a slow news day anymore, something momentous is always happening. Every day there appears to be a reason to run to the family room and turn on the radio or the telly to hear yet another breathless journalist attempting to communicate the unbelievable.

In years to come, when we are asked where we were when Trump's supporters invaded Capitol Hill and occupied the houses of Congress, we might remember it was the same night the third Covid lock-down was announced and not quite a week after the UK left the European Union.

We are just a few days into 2021 and already so much has happened. We thought 2020 was a year like no other but it is beginning to appear as if we are halfway through a two-year period like no other.

If we are not careful, we will run out of superlatives; infections are higher than they have ever been, hospitals more crowded than they have ever been and there are more people on social welfare than ever before. Everything seems to be over the top, and there's a whole eleven and a half months of the year left.

Will we be able for it? It is easy to become overwhelmed, or to allow oneself to be overwhelmed. I have a friend who suffers from a mild form of depression that occasionally takes a severe turn. It usually begins with something simple, like an unpaid bill he has let sit there for weeks, an item that would have been easy to attend to had he dealt with it at the time. Procrastination heaps itself on procrastination and demand notes build up and he conflates the failure to pay the bill with other failures and disappointments that have marked his life. Eventually he takes to the bed.

Then the dishes pile up in the sink, on the coffee table and on the bedside locker. The bin is overflowing with take-away cartons, the post piles up in the hall blocking the front door and, before he knows it, everything from his laundry basket to his is lawn is in absolute chaos. He buries himself under a heap of blankets, burrowing into the mattress hoping it will all go away.

His road to recovery begins the day he turns towards the kitchen on his way back from the bathroom, stands at the sink and washes the first cup. Slowly and incrementally small achievements build on one another until he is back to himself, having rediscovered his capacity for making decisions and following through on them.

Even though he is not an alcoholic his motto for recovery is the motto of Alcoholics Anonymous, 'one day at a time.' In fact, 'one step at a time' might more accurately describe the journey back to wellness and his escape from what Churchill used to call, 'the black dog'.

In the cool of his good times he can clearly describe his descent into the abyss of lethargy and despondence. It begins with what he calls 'a niggle' – an issue or a negative memory that gets under his skin. Unchecked, this leads to 'a gathering of the unresolved issues of his life' until he becomes overwhelmed and takes to the bed.

He is now well able to recognise the signs of impending trouble. He knows when to reach out for a shoulder to lean on as he seeks to avoid the whirlpool of negativity that threatens to draw him in and drag him down.

January is a month that can be overwhelming. The weather doesn't inspire, there is no season of tinsel and trinkets to look forward to and there will be many a cold breeze and bitter shower between it and the laughing yellows of April. With the addition of a mutating virus the month has a mean and a deadly streak.

In days like this it can be hard to fight the downward thrust of doom-laden superlatives. It is hard not be overwhelmed. My friend has learned how to manage by keeping his eyes on the nearest horizon, the one he knows he can get to if he takes it one day at a time.

'Today' is all that is real, and the demands of today are all he needs to manage. If the floor is covered in discarded clothes, picking up the first sock changes all that. If the bills are in a mound behind the door, opening the first envelope and making the first phone call changes everything. If the sink is heaped with dirty delph, washing the first cup breaks the downward momentum and marks a new beginning.

Be it in breakdown or lock-down, embracing one day at a time will eventually bring us to April and its bright promise.

# 8

# I was wrong to think I was wrong

There is many a week I sit in front of the screen with nothing to write about and nothing to say. Eventually the pressure of the ticking clock and the terror of the blank page will force one word to follow another until a collection gathers that might have the potential to be something decent.

If the aforementioned pressures and terrors aren't enough the current consort will appear in the scriptorium, bank statement in hand asking if I'm due to be paid any time soon. There is nothing like the amber light flashing over the bank account and the presence of a woman who knows her debits from her credits to concentrate the mind. It is certainly no time to mention writer's block, an affliction that elicits a level of disdain normally reserved for the man-flu.

There are times when there is lots to write about, but you don't know where to start you don't know if you should start and you are not sure if it's your place to say anything. This is one of those times.

The story of the mother and baby homes and the trail of human destruction left by the awful events of that time is heart-breaking and shameful.

President Higgins painted a fairly accurate picture of the institutional landscape that created the conditions for these things to happen. He says it is important to recognise "how a newly independent state was captured by a judgemental/authoritarian version of Church/State relations that sought to be the sole and ultimate arbiter of morality."

That whole period, from the foundation of the State to the 1990s, is characterised by a tyranny of certainty and a suppression of questioning, where the notion of mystery was itself used as a form of control.

My first few decades on the planet coincided with the last decades of that world, when the seasons of the ecclesiastical year marked the passage of time, where church feast days were public holidays and the sacred had precedence over the secular. The only uncertainty was the relationship between civil law and canon law, it was like a meandering and porous border where it was hard to know what jurisdiction you were in. This confusion suited the powers that be.

It was a time when there was no meat eaten on a Friday and no dances happened during Lent. Subjects like the intricate rules of fasting and abstinence were frequent topics of discussion on radio, television and in the newspapers.

A quirky story I remember from those days gives a sense of the kind of society that prevailed. Under the strictures of the Lenten fast a person could eat one full meal a day and two collations – two light meals. During a particularly harsh spring the then Bishop of Cork, Dr Cornelius (Connie) Lucey, responded to a request to relax the fast by granting permission for a biscuit to be consumed at one's tea break. With typical Cork ingenuity the local bakers produced jam biscuits the size of saucers and, in typical Corkonian fashion, the locals nicknamed them 'Connie Dodgers.'

It was a time when theologians were as likely to be consulted about social legislation as were members of the legal profession or politicians. I can remember a particularly strident professor of moral theology being asked if he had ever been wrong about anything. "Once," he said, "I was asked a question and I thought I gave the wrong answer. When I did my research I discovered I was right, so I was wrong to think I was wrong."

This straitjacket of absolute certainty left little room for the vagaries of the human condition. The milk of human kindness was seen as weakness and the veneer of universal compliance with social and religious norms was more important than the real needs of people, particularly women and their children.

Emotional, social, psychological and physical lives were crushed under the suffocating demands of outward propriety. There is no end to the damage that was done to people, particularly to women and their children in a world governed by a code of transactional morality overseen by a God painted into a transactional corner stripped of grace and graciousness.

In the dying decades of this dispensation, I got to know a group of people who had spent most of their lives in institutions similar to those referred to in the recent coverage. Some were religious and some residents, placed there as young people by family, church or state. They had all grown older together and had morphed into one community living out their remaining years gently and gracefully.

Freed of the tyranny of unrelenting certainty, peace had come softly, as it comes to all of us, through the undefined and mysterious margins of our humanity.

# 9

# The power of the word

It was a fine autumn afternoon in 1969, the schoolyard was full of whooping children enjoying the two-o-clock break. I should have been with them, but I was still in the classroom where yellow shafts of autumn sunshine beamed through the tall windows illuminating a galaxy of swirling dust particles.

I sat there trying to figure out why the Master had told me to stay behind. What had I done wrong? I was perplexed as I watched the tall, gaunt teacher walk down between the rows of desks carrying a big dictionary. He perched himself on the upper section of the desk in front of mine and opened the book on his lap, "Now James," he said, "you are good with words, always have a dictionary close at hand and, every day, learn a new word and its meaning."

While I can't say I followed his advice to the letter, his words and actions sank a deep well for me, a well I go back to again and again for reassurance and sustenance. More than fifty years later, words are still making a difference to me; stringing them together gives my life a sense of purpose and helps provide me and mine with food, heat and shelter.

Words make a difference and have certainly made a difference to me. I am privileged to work with them, to experience their power and their beauty.

In 2017 I had occasion to meet a group of Americans at a small tourist event I was involved in. Afterwards I found myself at table with a couple who, as soon as the conversation turned to politics, told me they were Trump supporters. We chatted about his election and how America was since he came to power. When I asked them about some of the more unsavoury things he said about people, about certain countries and about various situations around the world one of them responded, "Those are only words, just words, I wouldn't let them bother me, let's see what he does."

Actions might speak louder than words, but words matter and words make a difference. In fact, words can transform reality. During the UK referendum on EU membership one of the breakthrough moments for the Leave campaign came about when they hit on the winning slogan, 'let's take back control.' In fact, 'let's take control' was their working slogan but the insertion of the word 'back' transformed it and, one could say, transformed British and European history.

Before I get too global let me to return to a place bordering my own locality, to North Kerry. I have great regard for the wordsmiths of this particular haven of Hiberno-English where Bryan McMahon, Gabriel Fitzmaurice, John B Keane, Brendan Kennelly and Con Houlihan caught much of its beauty and whisked it into a delight.

A number of years ago, in the course of a television documentary about Con Houlihan, Brendan Kennelly recalled sending a draft of his first collection of poems to Con asking for advice, a comment and maybe even a blessing. He got a one-line response telling him, "You're making the right mistakes."

It reminds me of a north Kerry musician I knew, a man who could turn his hand to any instrument. Among his myriad of musical tools was a steel guitar imported from Memphis Tennessee. One of my friends asked him how long it would take someone to master it, the musician stared at the instrument, thought for a minute and said, "After six months you'd be awkward" – awkwardness being an improvement on uselessness.

Another man I knew from that neck of the woods was a born storyteller whose normal conversation would weave its way in and out among a series of interconnected stories. His stories were delivered in the gorgeously cavernous vowels and cliff-edge consonants of the North Kerry vernacular. Listening to him talk was like listening to a master chef describe every delicious morsel of a gourmet meal. He had a weakness for tangents, but always returned to his main thread.

I hadn't seen the man for years and on the phone one day to a mutual friend from Tralee I asked about him, "Oh he's fine," my contact said, "age is doing no harm to his vocal chords. He's a great man with words. I'll tell you something else, he's the only man I know who can interrupt himself."

Words are powerful conveyors of levity, hilarity, beauty, truth and elegance. They can also be powerful agents of nastiness and destruction driving men and women to the edge of foolishness and beyond.

Last Wednesday, standing in her yellow radiance in front of the imposing Capitol building in Washington, Amanda Gorman, a princess of poetry, spoke words of beauty, truth, elegance and power, sending waves of redemption cascading over the balustrades and down the steps that had lately witnessed so much hate.

# 10

# A drop of the good auld sup

A note from the ESB told us we would be without power for a few hours on Wednesday last. Even though we had time to prepare, when the outage happened the loss of electricity was keenly felt.

The moment the supply was cut off the computers went dark, the Wi-Fi stopped winking, the water dried up (we have our own well), and the central heating stopped. The stove in the living area had to remain unlit as it heats a back boiler, which would have exploded without a functioning circulation pump.

Luckily, we have a gas hob so we could boil a kettle and make tea. Thanks to a small stove in the sitting room, we at least had heat in one corner of the house.

Under normal circumstances the power-cut wouldn't have affected us. At the time it happened the students would have been at school and the current consort at work. I could have relocated to a 'hot desk' at the local business hub or thrown my wellies into the boot of the car and found a farm to walk in some part of the country.

But in these strange times we had no option but to sit it out in a house of dead computers, limited heating and fading mobile phones. To add to our misery the day was grey and damp and shrouded in a dense fog that hung over the place like a sodden blanket.

If all that wasn't enough, hopes of the imminent arrival of Covid vaccines were dashed as the number of doses expected from Astra Zeneca took a nosedive. According to the radio Ursula Von der Leyen was laying into the manufacturers but was getting little satisfaction.

The cumulative effect of the fog, the power cut and the bad news gave me a longing for a vaccination of hot whiskey and a dose of the bed.

Astra Zeneca, what a strange name? Sounds like something Captain Kirk and Dr Spock might have fretted about on the bridge of Starship Enterprise.

In a curious association of memories and musing, it struck me that when Star Trek first appeared on our snowy television screens the rural medicinal cabinet contained three staple remedies: Epsom salts, Sloan's Liniment and poteen.

Poteen was the original generic cure for ailments afflicting man and beast, capable of healing anything from diarrhoea to dropsy. It was generally stored in innocent-looking bottles designed to carry more mainstream beverages such as Nash's red lemonade or Mi-Wadi. The illicit distillation could equally be found camouflaged in bottles that had once contained a brand of legally distilled whiskey.

For years I stored a personal supply of the finest Rosenallis poteen in a gin bottle. I arrived home one evening to find the current consort and her sister in great form, enjoying what they thought was an 'interesting' gin and tonic.

In my original neck of the woods I remember hearing about a part-time farmer who came in from the pub one night to the unwelcome news that they had a 'cow down'. The animal was lying in the shed unable to stand. The man immediately changed into his strong boots, reached into the dresser for the bottle of poteen and, telling his wife not to wait up for him, set out to resurrect the sick cow.

Daylight was peeping over the horizon when the wife noticed his absence from the marital scratcher and, grabbing an overcoat, made her way straight to the shed. There she found the cow in an upstanding position calmly chewing the cud while her husband lay snoring on a bed of straw cradling an empty bottle. She roused him from his slumbers and asked him to explain himself. Propped up on his elbows he told her that when he came to the barn he administered half the bottle of poteen to the cow and, seeing how well it suited her, he administered the other half to himself. In an act of solidarity or stupor, he went down beside her. Surveying the scene the wife remarked, "I suppose it isn't all bad; you could say I'm a cow up and a man down."

Happily, for me, and the current consort, I didn't take to the bed or the hot toddies. The electricity came back sooner than expected and the computers whirred into life. We all returned to our desks and the house resounded once more to the clicks of mice and the clack of keyboards, the signature sounds of our Covid cottage industry.

We wish Frau Von der Leyen well as she strives to secure a steady supply of potions from the medicine men and women of the new frontier.

But, if all else fails, we can reach into the dark recesses of the old dresser, beyond the box of solidified Epsom salts and the bottle of coagulated Sloan's Liniment, to where the good old mountain dew, improving with age, stands ready to ease whatever ails us

# 11

# Retail terror

I shop for clothes once a year, and only wish my visits to the dentist were as infrequent. An afternoon during the January sales will find me in the drapery section of a small selection of stores kitting myself out for the twelve months ahead. When I return home with my bag of rags the current consort will invariably remark that it didn't take me too long. I'm a functional shopper, except when it comes to books; I could spend a whole day in a bookshop and come home with enough reading material to last two pandemics.

The concept of retail therapy is beyond me, why someone would shop for pleasure is an alien concept. Although I do remember once shopping therapeutically. I was having a particularly difficult time at work and, during lunchtime one day, I took myself to the local shopping centre to buy some lunch and escape from the office.

As I wandered around aimlessly munching on my ham and cheese roll, I spotted a pair of lovely Italian shoes on display in the window of a shoe shop. They were beautiful, with shiny black leather uppers and tan leather soles. After I finished my roll, I popped in to try them on. They slipped on to my feet as if they belonged there forever.

An attentive assistant was glowing in her assessment of how well they suited me. Unfortunately, the price tag put them beyond my reach. With three small children at home and a mortgage to pay I couldn't justify spending that kind of money on footwear. I handed them back to the assistant who put her head to one side and looked at me as if I was a sad puppy. She asked if I would like to try another, more economically sensitive brand, but it was the Italians or bust - nothing else would soothe my existential angst. I moped my way back to the grey walls of the workplace, resigned to spending the rest of my life in the mediocrity of leatherette and rubber.

However, a few weeks later the work situation improved dramatically. I felt like dancing and singing and buying Italian shoes, which I duly did. I called to the shop on my way home and the same sensitive assistant attended to me, insisting I try them on again. They fitted as neatly this time as they did previously and, with the delight of the footman who discovered Cinderella, she boxed and wrapped my Mediterranean footwear, we were both charmed with my purchase and agreed I was worth it.

As things turned out, the shoes were not as fond of me as I was of them. After a few outings to weddings, funerals and similar formal occasions the reality of their dislike dawned on me, painfully. My gorgeous sleek black Italians turned out to be a pair of straitjackets that seemed to tighten at every perambulation. I eventually gave them to a friend endowed with a more dainty pair of crubeens than me.

Had my dalliance with the Italians worked out I might now be an avid proponent of the therapeutic benefits of shopping, I might even have developed an online presence earning a fortune as an 'influencer'. Yes, an influencer for the golden oldies, advertising a range of comfortable clothes for those who need comfort rather than speed in all things. But alas and alack, the pair of elegant Mediterranean straitjackets choked off those possibilities before they had a chance to germinate.

The current consort shares my utilitarian approach to shopping. However, we have reared daughters who savour every element of the process. They smack their lips at the prospect of a trip to the shops going into a trance as they saunter their way through the aisles, stroking fabrics here, taking a sample spray of perfume there, holding garments up to their necks and flicking their hair back as they swivel in front of full-length mirrors trying to establish whether or not the item does anything for them.

There is a distinct sense of completion when they arrive at the checkout desk. Parting painlessly with card or cash they watch, mesmerised, while their latest acquisition is wrapped and bagged. And as they leave the emporium, arms draped in bags, they pause here and there for one last look at items that caught their eye but didn't quite make the shortlist. They touch them reassuringly as if to say, "I will be back for you, darling, just you wait."

In these lock-down days the shopping experience is reduced to a two-dimensional screen transaction – that is until the white van appears at the gate signifying that a full session of retail therapy is about to be delivered in one shot. As the driver slides open the side-door of his vehicle the excitement reaches fever pitch inside the house where shaking hands struggle with the lock on the front door. As the man approaches the porch the parcel is taken from him with the minimum of ceremony. After a whooping dash down the corridor the wrapping is torn open, the fabric is stroked, the garment is held up to the neck and the soothing effect of a full dose of retail therapy ripples through the house.

I'm happy to wait for the January sales.

# 12

# Has the wind come to stay?

After the pub, the forge was probably the most popular gathering spot for men in rural Ireland. At the forge you could laze around with legitimacy. Aside from the blacksmith nearly everyone was there to do nothing except wait; wait for a horse to be shod, the sock of a plough to be fitted, a gate to be straightened or rivets to be inserted.

There was no better place to go on a wet day, you'd be dry, warm and entertained to the glow of blacksmith's fire. You could even make yourself useful pumping the bellows when red heat was required. The conversation was always lively, peppered with wisdom, devilment and the occasional nugget of gossip.

The blacksmith often worked late into the evening, a time when he got a bit of space and peace once his farming customers went home to milk the cows. But there was no guarantee he would be left alone when the shadows lengthened, and the evening fell. After they ate the supper the men who worked nine-to-five jobs would saunter in for their sojourn around the blacksmith's fire. Arrayed in cardigan, collar and tie, with pipes full of tobacco and heads full of tales from the metropolis they would perch themselves within spitting distance of the glowing coals.

A certain member of the collar and tie brigade, who had the highest of regard for anything he had to say, was expounding one evening on the destruction wreaked by a recent storm. After detailing the physical mayhem from Cahersiveen to Carlingford Lough he asked the blacksmith if he had heard the wind.

"I did of course," the blacksmith replied, as he dropped a piece of red-hot iron into the cooling barrel where it hissed like a thousand snakes.

"Did you get up?" he was asked,

"I did not, I stayed in the bed listening to it," he said, "like I have to listen to you."

I was reminded of this story recently. In fact, I'm reminded of it most every night for the past few weeks as the wind howls against the roof causing rafters to creak and slates to shudder. Our sleeping quarters are located in the upstairs of a dormer house, close to the frontline when the wind launches assault after assault on anything that stands in its way. In a fit of irrational irritation I found myself, after the third or fourth consecutive night of gale force wind, getting cross with it as I tossed and turned asking aloud if the whistling, howling and lashing of rain on the skylight would ever stop.

According to many experts the increased frequency and severity of high winds and stormy conditions are a consequence of climate change. In a NASA blog from March 2020 Alan Buis, from NASA's Jet Propulsion Laboratory, tells us that "Earth's atmosphere and oceans have warmed significantly in recent decades. A warming ocean creates a perfect cauldron for brewing tempests. Hurricanes are fuelled by heat in the top layers of the ocean and require sea surface temperatures (SSTs) greater than 26° Celsius to form and thrive....Since 1995 there have been 17 above-normal Atlantic hurricane seasons…" While all scientists are not quite willing to hang their hats on the connection between climate change and the severity of storms, most agree that greater levels of precipitation are to be expected.

Closer to home, Maynooth's Professor John Sweeney, a member of the Intergovernmental Panel on Climate Change (IPCC), tells us that for every single degree of warming in the atmosphere there is a 7 per cent increase in water vapour. His colleague, Professor Peter Thorne goes on to explain that the atmosphere acts like "a leaky sponge" when warmed. Isn't well we know it.

Two words could describe our daily weather forecasts, wind and rain. Like the late blacksmith from my own village, I have no choice these nights but listen helplessly while gust after gust of wind tries its damnedest to peel something off my roof.

As I write this, I'm listening to my four-year-old young neighbour, who has broken out of the confines of his own garden and is running around mine, whooping with delight as he leads his father on a merry chase.

I wonder what will be here when he is my age, almost 60 years from now? Will his children and his grandchildren sit with him at night in a weatherproof capsule and ask, "What was the world like before the wind came to stay?"

# 13

# I might need a slipperectomy

The current consort and I have become so accustomed to our nightly commute from the dinner table to the television, I'm wondering if we will ever again want to leave the house after the dinner plates are deposited in the dishwasher.

In normal times, on any given night, at least one of us would be rushing out to a rehearsal, a show, a choir practice or a committee meeting of some kind.

When this is all over, we will have to be genetically reprogrammed, the slippers will have to be surgically removed and the sitting room door will have to be barred if we are to return to the way things were.

All joking aside, the world has changed and this lock-down is having a serious impact on people.

A friend of mine and her husband were out walking near their home recently, enjoying the crisp March air, when they stopped to greet a fellow walker. They knew him to see but never really met him. In the course of conversation, he told them they were the first people he had spoken to since Christmas.

Another friend visiting a garden shop last week was told by one of the assistants that, a few days previously, an elderly customer, while examining the roses on display outside, got a thorn stuck in her thumb. Without thinking, the assistant took her hand in his and extracted the thorn. "Oh," he said, "I shouldn't have done that." After assuring him there was no need to apologise, she told him he was the first human being to have touched her in a year.

Goodness knows what stories will emerge when this plague passes. But even before all this began a cultural and social phenomenon called 'the atomisation of society' was emerging as a sort of perverse outcome of mass communication. This creeping and insidious process, exacerbated by social media, is driving social isolation. It manifests itself in circles of friends and circles of belonging that are getting smaller and smaller, in some cases reduced to the immediate family or even to no one beyond the individual, himself or herself.

A priest friend of mine who ministered in a rural parish for most of his life found himself in later years in a city parish. He was amazed at the number of people living lives completely isolated from their neighbours and the broader community, whose houses or flats are like sealed units and whose needs are fed by take-aways and TV.

In Japan there are over 500,000 people known as 'hikikomori'. Variously described as shut-ins or latter-day hermits they hardly ever leave their houses or apartments. The phenomenon isn't particular to Japan, it is also evident in South Korea, Hong Kong, across the US and Europe. Some who opt for this lifestyle have a technology addiction but for many the demands of modern society have become too much.

The trend was recognised over quarter of a century by American political scientist, Robert D Putnam. In 1995 he published a thought-provoking essay, later expanded into a book, entitled *"Bowling Alone – The decline in America's Social Capital."* In both works he examined the decline in public participation and engagement in America. Using bowling as an example he pointed out that in the mid-1990s there were far more people bowling across America than 20 years previously, however, the numbers participating in bowling leagues had all but collapsed. People were bowling alone.

Putnam attributed the fall-off in public engagement to a multitude of factors, including work pressures, suburbanisation, commuting and generational change. He reckoned 25pc of the decline was due to the individualisation of media – meaning television. What would he make of the granular individualisation driven by social media, when the device in our hands predicts our preferences and has the power to lock us into our own echo chamber?

There is a great danger that among the outcomes of these difficult days will be a further atomisation of our society. While I have no doubt, but as soon as the vaccines get the upper hand and the lock-downs end there will be great fiestas of public engagement. I also fear that once we have completed our first round of handshaking and hugging, we will retreat to a default position of distance and self-isolation. Something in us will make us recoil from crowds and crowded places.

We will need time to practice walking together, sitting with one another and enjoying one another again.

# 14

## Rumblings in my gastronomic memory

Every now and again a cry goes up urging us to go back to basics, a move trumpeted as the antidote to everything that ails us.

I must confess to a recent longing to taste some of the basic foodstuffs I remember from my young life; simple things like buttered scones, jam and brown sauce, not all in the same dish, I might add. These are among the tastes that graced my palette as a youngster.

When I was growing up, mealtimes were the metronome that maintained the rhythm of the day. All things were scheduled around breakfast, dinner, 'the-four-o-clock' and supper. There were also minor break times. In some households mid-morning was marked by what posh people called 'elevenses', whereas many rural homesteads regarded the 'four o clock' as sacrosanct. On farms with a dairy herd, the afternoon collation was the important one, being the last bit, bite or sup one got until the cows were milked.

The 'four-o-clock' was the original rural take-away, transported from the kitchen to wherever the work was happening. Delivering the repast was the job of those not quite old enough to pike hay, sow spuds, drive a tractor or operate a chainsaw. Prior to being press-ganged into the world of 'real men's work', one had to serve one's time in the mobile catering department hauling the four-o-clock.

The light afternoon meal generally consisted of tea and home-made scones lathered in butter and topped off with jam. Sometimes there might be a few (buttered) slices of 'spotted dog', a type of soda bread speckled with raisins, (in some houses it was known as 'spotted dick', a name that, for obvious reasons, fell out of favour). The fare could also include fruitcake or barmbrack, depending on the time of year.

The tea was carried in whiskey bottles snuggled into thick woollen socks and corked with wedges of tightly rolled newspaper. The scones and cake were on a large dinner plate draped in a tea towel. It was no small feat for a pair of bony youngsters in short pants to carry all that food and drink, plus a few mugs, from one end of the farm to the other. There were no internal farm roads or sleek electric fences at that time. One had to haul the assortment of refreshments across cattle-poached fields and over stone walls, thick with profusions of briars and nettles at either side.

To add to the challenge, those of us selected for the fodder party were often late leaving the house and our mother would send us off with the injunction, "if ye fall don't wait to get up."

To sustain us on our odyssey to the outer reaches of the land, on occasion we found it necessary to commandeer some of the fare meant for the men. Depending on how far we were from our destination, there could be more than one raid mounted on the plate of goodies. We often arrived at our rendezvous with full bellies and a much-depleted store of supplies. When my father and grandfather would see the meagre pickings remaining on the plate one of them would ask, "Does your mother think tis a pair of snipes she's feeding?" We would try not to hiccup.

So, what took me on this journey back through the decades? Well, I was in the supermarket during the week and as I passed an array of baked goods my attention was drawn to a basket of scones. Although individually wrapped in cellophane, they looked delicious. Something rumbled deep in my gastronomic memory as I imagined one of them sliced in half, covered in butter and jam and smiling up at me.

As if possessed by some external force I picked up a pair of the soft, brown mounds of gorgeousness and made straight for the shelves containing the condiments and preserves. I quickly selected a pot of strawberry jam.

Still in a state of possession, as I passed a shelf lined with sauces and spices from Bangalore to Ballymaloe my nostalgia-stricken eyes spotted a simple bottle of Chef brown sauce. Remembering there was some cold beef in the fridge the ultimate supper began to take shape in my head; sliced tomatoes, a few slices of the current consort's brown bread, slivers of beef and a spoonful of brown sauce on the side – what more could a country boy ask for?

Such feasting; with the scones and jam I had the makings of the classic four-o-clock, a few short hours later, the cold beef and brown sauce would make for the perfect supper.

Grabbing the bottle of Chef by the neck I deposited it in the basket with the rest of my retro fare and headed for the checkout in full mid-twentieth century mode. I almost expected to pay for it in shillings and pence.

When I got home and set my purchases down on the kitchen table the current consort looked at them, looked at me and wondered if I had become stuck in existential reverse, "The next thing you'll be wearing short pants," she said.

"You wish," I replied, "put on the kettle, my little cowslip, we're going back to basics."

# 15

# Punctuality – nature or nurture?

Punctuality is much regarded in highly organised societies. There is great admiration for the man or the woman 'you could set your clock by'.

In agricultural circles there are certain farms where the rhythm of life is metronomic in its adherence to time, where even the cows know what time to come home. On other farms you could find the cows in the parlour at any time of the day or night, in such places they refer to the 'first and second' milking rather than the 'morning and evening' milking.

My mother had a loose relationship with the clock. In fact, when we'd make arrangements to meet our cousins they'd ask if the time of our arrival was set in accordance with Greenwich Mean Time or 'Aunty Eily time'. It's hard to blame the poor woman for rejecting the tyranny of the clock; the needs of a clatter of children and a heap of farm work had to be squeezed into every hour and minute of the day.

I remember once, as she hooshed us into Sunday mass after a journey from home that would leave Niki Lauda breathless, a man behind us said, "You know you're late when the O'Briens are going in ahead of you."

I think I inherited my mother's relationship with time. In one of my previous existences, I worked in Italy as a tour guide where I dealt with Irish tourists, Italian hoteliers and Austrian coach drivers. I broke the Austrians' hearts at our various stops along the way. Leading my merry band of tourists from the bus I would arrange with the drivers the time and place for the pick-up. The chauffeurs would invariably raise their Tyrolean eyebrows and ask if the arrangements were in accordance was Irish time or Swiss time.

I developed something of a reputation for cutting things fine when it came to punctuality, and tended not to disappoint. That was until the current consort came along. Our contrasting relationships with the clock continues to be the cause of many a skirmish. She claims she was never late for anything until she met me, and I admit was never on time for anything until I met her.

As an example, one of the many things she discovered about me after we threw in our lot together was that I have an ongoing minor health issue that is of little consequence once it is regularly monitored. This involves a brief six-monthly check up. When she learned I was five years late for my last appointment I was dispatched post haste to Dublin and haven't missed an appointment since. It was never her intention to hitch her wagon to a self-destructive crock.

Of course, those with a reputation for punctuality are not necessarily virtuous in every other respect. After 20 years in power the only good thing Italians could find to say about Benito Mussolini was that he made the trains run on time.

Closer to home I'm reminded of the moment, on January 16, 1922, when the British Viceroy, Lord FitzAlan prepared to hand over Dublin Castle to the new Irish Free State in the person of Michael Collins. FitzAlan is reputed to have chastised Collins for being seven minutes late. To which Collins is supposed to have replied, "After 700 years we won't begrudge you the seven minutes." Many doubt this exact exchange took place since Collins and his colleagues from the Provisional Government were in fact an hour and a half late for the ceremony.

While some claim punctuality is a quality one is born with, others say it's a habit that requires nurture and a discipline that takes a certain amount of rigour to impose.

It might come as a surprise to learn that the great Mahatma Gandhi was the ultimate stickler for time. Believing the wise and disciplined use of time to be a moral imperative, he regarded it as a precious gift and not ours to waste. He lived by his watch and obeyed a very strict timetable, a practice he believed kept him free from distraction and enabled him to be completely present to whatever task was timetabled for that moment.

When he was assassinated, among his few earthly possessions was a watch attached to his garments by safety pin and string. The watch stopped the moment he was shot.

I was contemplating all these things when the current consort enquired as to what I was writing about this week,

"Punctuality," I answered.

"What, pray tell, would you know about it?" she asked.

I was tempted to quote Evelyn Waugh who described punctuality as 'the virtue of the bored,' but I didn't, did I?

# 16

# No room for rumination

For the procrastinator tomorrow is a great day, but sometimes it comes too soon.

I have been talking about getting the exterior of the house painted for about 12 months. During the first lock-down I had intended to press my daughters into service but a friend, who knows about these things, dissuaded me saying the first painting of a new house should be done by someone who knows something about it and he recommended a good tradesman for the job.

He also warned me that sending inexperienced youngsters up ladders with paint tins, brushes and rollers isn't the best idea in the world.

My friend's advice played to my predilection for procrastination, and I postponed the job. I must admit I had occasional bouts of second thoughts throughout the summer as I watched these able-bodied lassies hanging around with nothing to do and a house screaming to be painted.

I was their age, or thereabouts, in the summer of 1977. On August 16 of that year, I was on a ladder on a galvanise roof slathering it with red oxide paint. The date is etched in my memory because it was the day Elvis died. One of my sisters came out of the house and rebroadcast what she had just heard on the radio. I can remember the commentators remarking on how tragic it was that, at 42 years of age, he should have died so young. From the perspective of a 19-year-old perched on a shed in west Limerick Elvis was old.

Let me get back to paint and procrastination. Earlier this spring the exterior painting of the house climbed back up the domestic agenda and, after much prodding from the current consort, I spoke to the man recommended by my friend and he agreed to do the job in May. Herself chose the colour scheme and I was tasked with making the place ready.

As March turned to April the window of opportunity for getting my designated tasks done narrowed. I began to contemplate the acquisition of a power washer and noticed my neighbour using one. I was gently psyching myself up for what lay ahead.

However, one evening last week my protracted period of contemplation and remote preparation was thrown into complete disarray. I got a text from the painter asking if I had acquired paint, I phoned him immediately thinking there had been some mistake. He said it suited him to come the following morning, otherwise I could be waiting for months.

There was no time for rumination. Even an inveterate old procrastinator like me knows there are certain opportunities in life you don't put off such as the early arrival of a plumber or a painter. In the course of the phone conversation I admitted I had no power-washing done but he assured me a decent hosing down of the walls would suffice. Anywhere I found discolouration I should scrub it with diluted bleach, particularly the windowsills. Noticing the panic in my voice he said I could wait a few weeks if I wanted to, but the weather forecast was good for the coming days.

I had no choice but grasp the moment, "Tomorrow is fine," I said, with all the enthusiasm of someone confirming a dental appointment.

"Grand," he replied," I'll be there at 8 o clock, but you need to hose the place down this evening in order for it to be dry."

I swung into action. The current consort suggested that the hosing shouldn't take too long but we agreed the state of the footpaths was a different story, they were covered in five years of grime and would look atrocious beneath freshly painted walls. I went to my trusty neighbour and borrowed his power washer.

Using the ordinary garden hose, I washed down the walls and enlisted herself to give a hand scrubbing the sills, some of which were red with discolouration. It was nearly 9pm by the time I got to power-washing the footpaths and carried on until darkness fell and the neighbours' need for sleep prevailed.

I was back out at cockcrow the following morning blasting away and cursing the lumps of moss and lichen that seemed to be superglued to every surface. My man arrived at 8am to find me grinding my way around the house in a fog of spray.

He took pity of me and went to the hardware store to collect the paint. As soon as he returned and began painting, I finished the last few bits, crawled upstairs and fell into the shower.

Each aching muscle and every creaking bone reminded me that I am now one-and-a-half times the age Elvis was when he died.

As I admire the excellent job, completed early and at speed, I'm left to contemplate two lessons; the only cure for procrastination is 'now', and power-washing, like rock'n'roll, is not for old men.

# 17

# My legacy will be a thing with strings

There was a time when the only legacy that mattered was one that could be calculated in acres of land or bundles of cash. Mercifully, we live at a time when what you leave behind is calculated in a wide range of currencies. While I sometimes wonder what my children will inherit, aside from my neuroses and bad habits, I prefer to believe their lives will be full of their own promise, seasoned with a sprinkling of what they got at home.

I've been playing the guitar and eating my nails since I was 12. I was a first year in the Brideshead of my youth in East Cork where, every Saturday afternoon, a music teacher would come to the school. Budding musicians lined up outside the music room waiting to take their turn at trying the poor woman's patience.

To play guitar it is important to maintain short fingernails, in particular on the hand that presses the strings to the fretboard. Our music teacher would get quite annoyed if her guitar students hadn't attended to their manicuring before each lesson. She clearly did not understand that the life of a twelve-year old can be exceedingly busy with little time for doing one's nails. Most Saturdays, just about to go in to the music room I'd realise the talons on my left hand exceeded regulation length. Since I didn't carry a manicure set on my person, I had no option but to pare them back with some dental assistance.

Fifty years later I continue to play the guitar and, thankfully, have given up the nail biting bit. Except when I'm unexpectedly called on to perform and have to adopt emergency measures.

As I became a more confident player I would often end up in the engine room of singsongs in the local pub. One night an old fiddler said to me, "Youngfella, let me tell you, that contraption you're playing will keep you out all night." And he was right. While I'm no Christy Moore, Steve Cooney or Ed Sheeran, when it comes to traditional singsongs I can rise a sweat and pump out albums of songs where quantity and volume trump quality and subtlety. I have often played from sundown to sunrise climbing into bed leaving the birds and their dawn chorus to take up where I finished.

The guitar has been good to me, like the old John Denver song it introduced me to some friends of mine from Ballyculhane to Ballykenny, from Abbeyfeale to Aubais, from Kinnitty to Kent, from Eutin to Illinois and from Ballinagleragh to Ballywilliam. I was even introduced to 'Pearl the Girl from Erril' via the lungs of a man who is huge in Rathdowney. The guitar has been like a passport, a plane ticket and a train ticket.

Of course, like all good friends, there were times it could be a pain and an encumbrance. It was inclined to get above itself becoming the focus of attention. Indeed, some invitations to parties and functions should have been addressed to the instrument, "Dear Guitar, please bring Jim." However, the blessings it brought, the doors it opened and the friendships it nurtured far outweigh any blisters it might have caused to body, mind or soul.

Of late, my youngest offspring has surreptitiously taken an old guitar of mine to herself and, with the help of YouTube tutorials and a passion for music, she's causing me no end of quiet delight. At first, I pretended not to notice, there is nothing like the unbounded enthusiasm of a parent to put a halt to a child's tentative steps in a new direction. I couldn't resist eavesdropping and would find any excuse to linger in the vicinity of her playing, tip-toeing away if I felt I was smothering the flame.

One day I plucked up the courage to suggest a chord progression, on another occasion I mentioned a song that might be worth learning. Then I started to hear the strains of tunes from my ancient playlist; Joni Mitchell's 'Both Sides Now', Paul Simon's 'Kathy's Song', a ballad I got from an old friend in Fermanagh called the 'Lakes of Coolfin'. God forgive her, she even knows all the words to Don McLean's 'American Pie', a song that can cause the guards to be called to the most civilised of parties.

One night recently, with a glass or two of wine on board, I handled my own guitar, snuck in to where she was strumming and joined her for a gentle session of soft ballads.

In the case of one of my children, I'm beginning to understand that legacy is a thing with strings.

Thankfully she brings to the craft her own subtlety and grace – and a set of nail clippers.

# 18

# The joy of the jab

Getting vaccinated was a profound experience. I was surprisingly moved by it. Maybe I'm getting soft in my dotage, but there is something extraordinary in the human response to this pandemic.

The process began for me on the morning of Saturday, April 24. I was sitting in the kitchen with the radio on, enjoying the first coffee of the day, when I heard the public announcement encouraging those of my vintage to register online for our vaccination. I went straight to the computer, logged on to and clicked on all the required boxes until the screen told me I'd be sent a text message with my appointment.

By the following Friday I had heard nothing and began to wonder if I had missed a crucial box in the course of my clicking. I phoned the helpline where a kindly woman from the HSE confirmed I was registered, all I had to do was wait for a text giving me the time and place.

The next morning being Saturday, the current consort and I were sitting up in the scratcher scrolling through our phones and wondering which of us was going to be the first to get up and brew the coffee. Among my overnight texts messages I found one telling me to present myself at the Radisson Hotel on Monday morning at 11.35 for my AstraZeneca vaccination.

I jumped out of the bed, headed for the kitchen and returned 10 minutes later with a pot of coffee, a pair of cups, and a few slices of buttered brown bread topped off with our neighbour's home-made marmalade.

"Hmm," says she, "you should get vaccinated more often."

Monday came around quickly and, on the advice of people in the know, I took two paracetamol before I left the house for the vaccination centre. It was a cold, miserable, wet and windy day, not a good one for standing in line. I shouldn't have worried. There was no hanging about, from the moment I joined the cars snaking their way along the short driveway to the hotel carpark everything kept moving.

Volunteers, army personnel, medical professionals, members of the civil defence, along with part-time and full time HSE staff guided me from the carpark to the queue, met me at the door, confirmed I was in the right place at the right time and showed me exactly where to go next. Everyone was in the best of good humour.

With the minimum of fuss and no paperwork I quickly found myself at the door of the vaccination hall, where people were moving in and out of white cubicles like clockwork.

I was guided to a cubicle where two vaccinators, Ann and Marie were ready for me. "Now James, it's your turn" they said. All of a sudden, I couldn't speak, I was filling up to cry. Thank goodness for the face-mask and the fact the two women were busy preparing the accoutrements, I had a chance to compose myself.

The wonder of the thing suddenly dawned on me. My mind went back to March 2020 when a GP friend of mine, visibly upset, told me she was afraid most of her older patients would be taken by the virus. Fourteen months later and it looks like a corner has been turned.

As I sat there loosening my shirt, the extraordinary time we had been through seemed to telescope itself into these few moments. It felt as if the fragility of human existence and the wonder of human ingenuity were coming face to face in these small white spaces.

Ann and Marie took me through the ins and outs of the vaccine, confirmed my consent and, before I knew it, the deed was done. I thanked them profusely as I pulled on my shirt. They advised me to take two more paracetamol when I got home and, handing me a card with details of my vaccination, said I'd be called again in 12 weeks. They directed me to the waiting area where I was to sit and rest for 15 minutes in case there were any instant reactions.

As those of us who had just been vaccinated waited, young women went among us offering glasses of water and cleaned the vacated seats. People sat in silence with their coats on their laps looked around, absorbing this hive of human goodness. It was like that quiet period after communion when believers take a moment to reflect on the wonder and mystery of what has happened.

On the way home the car radio carried heart-breaking accounts of Covid's rampage through India. Is it too much to hope that human ingenuity might meet an abundance of justice, compassion and generosity?

It's not over at all, until it's over for all.

# 19

# From here to Clare on a Ferguson 65

These days everyone is on a 'journey'. Whether writing a book, converting the farm to organics, letting the hair go white or potty-training a dog, the 'journey' is sure to be 'absolutely amazing'.

As a metaphor for the change process it's as worn as a Roman road, but it isn't a bad one. A journey takes you out of yourself, away from the familiar and opens up the senses to all kinds of new experiences and possibilities.

A couple I once knew, whose children were grown and gone, would regularly take a day to go on what they called 'a school tour'. "When we'd get tired of looking at one another we'd travel to find other people to look at," the woman explained to me.

Along the way they tried to meet as many people as they could. They picked up hitch hikers to find out who they were, where they were coming from, where they were going to and who their mother was. If they went into a pub, they made sure it was at a quiet time in the afternoon when they'd have the landlord or landlady to themselves. At dinner and supper they interviewed the waiters and waitresses and any guests who happened to be located at a table within earshot or shouting distance.

When they were fed, found and full of news they'd return home with enough to talk about until the next time they got tired of looking at one another.

Journeys heighten the senses and sharpen the powers of observation alerting the traveller to the most minute of details. I remember as a young lad I drove a tractor from Kildimo in Co Limerick to Liscannor in Co Clare. The trusty Ferguson 65 had become surplus to requirements so, it was 'put on the paper' where it sold to a Liscannor farmer living 50 miles away on the shores of the Atlantic. As part of the deal my father agreed to deliver the machine but hadn't considered how he was going to fulfil that part of the bargain. I solved the problem by volunteering to drive the tractor to Clare.

I had a soft spot for the old Ferguson. Earlier that summer he had loaned it to me, along with a finger-bar mower, and I hired myself out topping fields and cutting rushes for the princely sum of £3 an acre.

I was in mid-contract on a local estate when 'his lordship' arrived from across the water for his annual visit. While touring the property he pulled up in the Land Rover to chat to me and was effusive in his praise of my kindness and generosity. When he returned to the yard and was told by his steward that these excellent qualities of mine were costing him £3 an acre, me and my beloved Ferguson were shown the gate.

At the end of August, with the hay in, the silage pit sealed, and the deal done for the sale of the tractor I mounted my faithful steed for the last time, facing her east for Limerick before turning northwest for Liscannor. After passing through Limerick I was progressing steadily along the dual carriageway to Shannon when the skies opened. With no cab and no protection from the elements every drop of rain seemed as big as a small bucketful and aimed directly at me. I stopped at Durty Nellies in Bunratty to get some rest and sustenance. I also needed to empty my trousers, an operation that is not quite as indelicate as it sounds. I was wearing waterproofs, but the rain flowing down over my jacket was lodging under my rear end in the tractor seat. Some of the run-off was penetrating the 'waterproofs' and so, when I dismounted, a gallon of water flowed down the back of my legs and into my shoes.

Durty Nellies was dark and warm and smelled of turf smoke, tobacco, porter, garlic and oxtail soup. I went all exotic and had myself a bowl of creamy, oily chowder. Suitably fortified and somewhat less wet I came out to find the weather had worsened. I tilted the seat forward to empty it of rainwater before easing myself into position.

Turning the key, the Perkins engine purred into life and I continued north west through Newmarket-on-Fergus, Clarecastle, Ennis, Inagh, Ennistymon and Lahinch, not stopping until I drove into the new owner's yard.

As soon as I arrived my father drove into the yard after me. We were invited for tay and scones, the tractor was paid for, the new owner got £5 for luck, and I got £10 for 'my troubles' and my wet arse. On the way home my father said, "Jamesie, that's a journey you'll never forget." He was right.

On a recent trip to the beach at Lahinch in the company of the current consort and the baby of the bunch, I recalled my rain-soaked 50-mile trip on the cab-less tractor. They agreed the journey must have been "absolutely amazing."

# 20

# Rebuilding Pompeii as Vesuvius rumbles

There are times when even the Good Book despairs of the world and the capacity of humans to change.

"All things are wearisome, more than one can say. The eye never has enough of seeing, nor the ear its fill of hearing. What has been will be again, what has been done will be done again; there is nothing new under the sun."

This passage is from the Book of Ecclesiastes, part of what is called the 'Wisdom Literature', a beautiful and poetic section of the Bible. While there is much in it that is joyous and life-giving, it doesn't shirk from naming some harsh realities.

The most recent eruption of hostilities between the Israelis and the Palestinians brought the above quotation to mind, along with the simmering signs of bother in relation to the Northern Ireland Protocol – the more things change the more they stay the same.

It can be depressing, how we go in endless circles with so many issues and problems that remain unresolved.

Housing is one that rarely leaves the headlines: it has bedevilled the country forever. During the Famine poor housing with atrocious living conditions exacerbated the calamity and acted as an accelerant in the spread of sickness and disease.

This was followed by the clearance of lands and mass evictions as unwanted tenant families were literally thrown out on the side of the road all over the country. By the turn of the century the overcrowded tenements of Dublin with their accompanying poverty gave the city an infamy it deserved.

After independence, while some admirable public housing schemes were undertaken, the issue remained problematic. I remember as a boy seeing an edition of Hall's Pictorial Weekly on TV featuring a man, a hearse builder by trade, who was reduced to living in one of his hearses for want of a roof.

During the Celtic Tiger years housing dominated the consciousness of the nation. Everyone and her father tried to get in on the act, people were queuing overnight to buy houses and apartments off the plans. In fact, some people were paying others to queue for them.

The abiding icon of the lean years after the crash was the skull and skeleton of the half-finished house in the half-built ghost estate. These places were like latter-day versions of Pompeii, with discarded yellow vests hanging from rusted scaffolding and upturned hard hats littering the uneven ground in evidence of lives suddenly disrupted.

From the perspective of our housing and homelessness problems those abandoned estates are a perversity. As the wind and rain blew through their windowless shells the levels of homelessness rocketed. Even when the broader economy appeared to be on the way up the number of people able to afford a home of their own declined steeply. We have now reached a point where the cost of rent is beyond those on average and lower incomes.

It took the sudden arrival of a pandemic to prove that everything from homelessness to our two-tier health service can be taken in hand. It proved that where there's political will, a way will be found. The state can extend its reach when it wants to.

Nevertheless, housing continues to be the great untouchable, for some reason the traditional political parties are desperately afraid to grasp the housing market and shake it to the core. They prefer to fiddle at it from a distance using stamp duty and capital gains tax like prosthetic extensions to the limbs of government. Meanwhile, they are quite willing to let ordinary people, especially the young, suffer everything from destitution to unrelenting uncertainty when it comes to fulfilling that basic of needs, the need for shelter.

Among the great sins of the Celtic Tiger years was the sin of deception; it deceived people into believing their houses are assets to be leveraged and sweated rather than homes to be lived in. So long as this deception continues to prevail the provision of housing will be a casino where the privileged and opportunists play roulette with everyone else's money.

The traditional political parties would be well advised to listen deeply to the young, to the generation that went into exile after the last crash and came back only to find that home ownership is beyond their reach.

The politicos would also be well advised to listen to the members of the next generation who came of age in the pandemic. The experience proved to them how relative everything is, that the sacred cows of the market can be de-consecrated and the state has far more power to shape society than it was willing to admit.

In the privacy of the polling booth these young citizens will give a far different slant to their pens than the one their parents gave. While the focus of much mainstream politics is on rebuilding Pompeii into what it once was, the young are rumbling impatiently in a nearby Vesuvius, waiting to erupt. They have different plans.

# 21

# Old stock

When acquaintances of my own vintage unexpectedly appear out of the dim and distant, I'm generally surprised at how much they have aged. I'm sure they have the same reaction when they see me. I suspect everyone regards themselves as ageless.

My self-image is stuck somewhere in the mid-forties. Even in the face of clear evidence that time is taking a toll on the body, I prefer to remain in denial. When the doctor tells me I should begin to expect 'this kind of thing' at my age, I smile and nod, convinced she is talking about someone else.

Denial is not necessarily a bad thing; it can help one deal with the ravages of time. However, denial can become delusion. Such delusion is often found in men who insist on playing contact sports when they are old enough to be a danger to their opponents, their teammates and themselves. Anyone who knows their Gaelic games will know that the ancient 'Junior' hurler makes up with guile and dirt what he lacks in speed and agility. Many the youthful, nippy forward finds himself limping off the field shortly after a close encounter with a Jurassic corner back.

I know of a man in his mid-fifties who found himself in the local A&E department after sustaining an ankle injury while playing five-a-side soccer. As he was discharged with his foot encased in plaster the nurse attending him, who was a neighbour, listed out the do's and don'ts of managing an ankle injury.

"Finally, Tom," she concluded, "you should trade in the football boots for a pair of hiking boots and a single bed."

"Why?' he asked

"From now on," she explained, "you'd be well advised to confine yourself to non-contact sports."

On the other extreme you have young people who long for venerability and are determined to get old before their time. They like to imagine they have spent far more time on the planet than the dates on their birth certificates attest to. I may be wrong, but I reckon females are not as predisposed to this condition as males.

These rare and exotic creatures, from the age of 12, adopt the practice of easing themselves in and out of chairs. By the time they reach 17 they've developed a slight stoop and walk with their hands behind their backs. As they get older they greet the arrival of gout, arthritis and lumbago as if they were lifetime achievement awards.

Their dress code includes braces, waistcoats and large handkerchiefs into which they blow their noses with much frequency, great volume and elaborate ceremony. They would drive a Morris Minor if they could find one and are wont to address friends and colleagues as "my dear man" or "dear boy". Once they pass 25, they can take to pipe-smoking or snuff sniffing and like nothing better than listening to themselves dispensing words of dubious wisdom from the shallow depths of an imaginary life.

This early longing for venerability is a recognised condition. In places where reincarnation is accepted as an article of faith people who exhibit these characteristics are referred to as 'old souls', reincarnated souls bringing with them the wisdom and attitudes they developed in previous incarnations.

However, I would be inclined to agree with those who describe the condition as a delusional attachment to an idealised era whose time has passed. Tridentine Mass enthusiasts along with their young, behatted and berobed clerics come to mind.

What brought all this on? Of late I have been contemplating the challenge of gracefully embracing a life where the days are increasingly bookended by supplements and suppositories. It isn't easy to carry on with some modicum of dignity while the laws of gravity play mollybawn with your wobbly bits.

Of course, there are days that are good, when age is but a number on a page. There are others that are not so good, when that ache in your lower back says it all. A few days ago, I was in the car with my learner driver daughter. We were leaving a petrol station and she stopped to make sure nothing was coming from right or left. The motorist behind us hooted impatiently much to the chagrin of my young pilot.

"Listen to that auld fella," she said, "he has no manners."

"How do you know he's an auld fella?" I asked.

"I saw him getting into his car," she said.

The hooting motorist followed us to the nearby roundabout where he drew up alongside. I turned to have a good look only to discover that the 'auld fella' was about twenty years younger than myself.

"He's not old," I said.

"Oh my God, Dad, he's at least forty."

That wasn't a good day.

# 22

# From long-john to sarong

It's summer, or so I'm told. Up to recently, it was hard to believe we would ever see the season again such was the cut of the wind and the Siberian edge to the temperatures. One of my abiding memories of May 2021 will be the sight of a herd of cows heading for a hedge to shelter from a murderous shower of hailstones. The old saying that 'a wet and windy May fills the barns with corn and hay,' wasn't predicated on the wind being polar.

The weather in Ireland can be exasperating but at least it gives us something to talk about. I wonder do the inhabitants of other parts of the world go on about it to the same extent Irish people do?

There are some indications they might. The Scots, for instance, are equally exposed to the hazards and vagaries of the wild Atlantic and keep a close eye on all things meteorological. A Scots thesaurus completed in 2015 claims our bekilted Celtic cousins have 421 words for snow. For our part, we Irish certainly have no shortage of words to describe rain and how it falls – bucketing, pouring, raining cats and dogs, pelting, misting, dribbling, drizzling, driving. Indeed, the most common verb used for intense rainfall is also used for urination.

Living with changeable weather is like living with a cantankerous relative, everything depends on the humour he or she is in today.

In that regard I have a friend who was married to a most unpredictable man. Thankfully his unpredictability had nothing to do with temperament or mood swings, it had to do with his multi-directional career path. He changed jobs as often as some people changed their socks. As a result, the financial and economic story of his life and that of the family was as undulating as a Monaghan farm.

One hare-brained moneymaking scheme followed another. The house was re-mortgaged a few times, but, luckily, his wife had a steady job ensuring there was food on the table and the children were educated. The man himself died at a relatively young age leaving a CV that stretched to volumes.

A few months after the funeral her sister came to visit. Reflecting on the life of the departed husband the visiting sibling suggested that, in hindsight, she should have married a different childhood sweetheart. The sweetheart in question grew into a man with a permanent pensionable job and a railroad-straight career signposted by key milestones like superannuation, points on the scale, annual leave, graded promotion and a lump sum.

"Maybe you're right," she said, "but we'd have had nothing to talk about."

If we didn't have the weather we'd have nothing to talk about. In the course of my own undulating career, I have spent time abroad in places where the weather is as predictable as a career in the Department of Agriculture, where the sun shines from dawn to dusk. The odd thunderstorm might briefly disturb the predictable pattern, but aside from that it is scorchio, scorchio, scorchio all the way.

On these sun-drenched costas where one blistering day melts into another there is little to inspire communal conversation. The only variety is to be found in the knobbly nature of the knees hanging below the shorts and the various states of curvature of the bodies inside the T-shirts.

While our capricious weather is the spark that ignites a billion conversations, more importantly, it makes us eminently adaptable, eternally optimistic and devoid of despair. We are relatively free of existential angst, an inevitable by-product of clockwork predictability.

Our weather has made us a people of great hope, we have wardrobes and garages bulging with the accoutrements of outdoor living that are more appropriate for a lifetime of summers in Provence. All we need is the hint of a heatwave and, in a matter of minutes, we go from long-john to sarong, from thermal to thong, from bacon to burrito and from Murmansk to Mediterranean.

As soon as the sun winks at us the roads fill up with convertible cars, our backyards are transformed into chiringuitos, garden furniture is assembled and barbeque grills are fired up sending smoke signals to the heavens. Even the parish priest shakes off the austere black and emerges from the presbytery in straw hat, Hawaiian shirt, Bermudas and Jackie Onassis sunglasses.

As those patches of blue that we like to call the sky become the dominant atmospheric variant we are transformed and reborn. Despite millennia of evidence to the contrary, we are confident it will never rain again.

# 23

# Waiting for a wedge

Writing is a bit like cycling a bike; you put one foot on a pedal and propel yourself along with the other until you have sufficient propulsion to throw your leg over the frame and land on the saddle. Sounds fairly simple, but there are days when, from the beginning, you're facing a steep hill and it takes a massive effort to generate enough speed to even attempt reaching the saddle. When you do, the bike can wobble along at a dangerously low speed as the steep incline conspires to turn you back into a pedestrian.

I often sit down to write, and it feels like I'm facing Everest on a high nelly with soft tyres. Inspiration can be about as plentiful as corncrake feathers. However, I rarely admit to being barren of thought or devoid of spark, I don't even tell the current consort in case it triggers a flood of suggested topics. Even a trickle of suggestions can smother rather than mother.

When faced with the blank page and the sense of panic rising like bile in my throat, the last thing I need is to find myself buried under a heap of possible ideas. In this state I don't have the capacity or the time to separate the exciting from the boring or the languorous from the libellous.

I'm not saying suggestions are unwelcome, indeed they are, but they are not instant solutions, they need time to mature in the dark recesses of the consciousness and the day will come when they are needed to do their bit. People who write, be it doggerel or high literature, never discard anything they come across. They will accept, borrow or pilfer stories, whispers, idiosyncrasies, foibles or feelings in the service of a craft where nothing is lost and everything will eventually have its use.

There's a man I meet on occasion who likes to quiz me about my scribblings. He is particularly curious about the people and incidents that populate the tales I tell from my youth. Being familiar with the country I come from he wonders why I don't write about certain other events that happened, or might have happened, or were purported to have happened in that corner of the planet. I shudder at some of the things he encourages me to write about, if I took them on board I could find myself alone and abandoned on the steps of the High Court.

I am reminded of the late actor and comedian, Niall Toibín, who regularly found himself the target of unsolicited stories. I once heard him describe meeting a man in a pub one night who had spent years waiting for the opportunity to tell the comedian a story that would 'suit him down to the ground'. From the first word the yarn was beyond bawdy, it would rise a blush on the cheeks of Lucifer. When the teller triumphantly delivered the lewd punchline he nudged Toibín and said, "Clean that up and you can tell it anywhere you like." Toibín nodded politely but knew in his heart and soul the only way to 'clean that up' was to never tell it again.

When times are really tough, and the muses are nowhere to be found every suggestion will be examined for merit. If this fails, I can be tempted to press the big red button, which means ringing the editor and asking if, by any chance, she has a picture of a big Simmental bull that would fit across four columns and fill a half page. Perhaps there is enough bull on this page already, without adding to it.

It is best to say nothing to anybody, to be desperate in silence, the very desperation can quarry the words from the rock-face of the mind and the pits of memory. Indeed, quarrying might be a better metaphor to explain the process of word smithing, especially when it comes to making use of suggestions.

Before the arrival of jackhammers, kango hammers or rock breakers, a very simple technology was applied in rock-breaking and quarrying. Lines of wooden wedges were driven into cracks in the stone, these were then soaked in water causing them to expand until the rocks or the rockface cracked even further, enabling a section to breakaway.

Recommendations, suggestions, stories and anecdotes are the wooden wedges in the process of writing; there will come a time when a fissure in the rock will be the exact fit for them. A few hours of punching into place at the keyboard, a generous dousing of imagination followed by a touch of intrigue and the job is done – at least until next week.

# 24

# A tip and an iceberg

I have never seen an iceberg, but if you are lucky or unlucky enough to catch a glimpse of one, I believe what you see is only a tenth of what you get. Ninety per-cent of any iceberg is under the water. Humans are the same, what we see and experience about one another is only a fraction of what is going on below the surface.

The exception of course is the so-called reality TV show, 'Love Island', where exposing as much of the private and personal as possible is the point of the exercise – along with the promise of instant fame and an improved bank balance.

Most people I know, myself included, talk to themselves. I would safely say that nearly all human beings have an incessant internal conversation going on. The amount of external conversing we do is but a fraction of this. The iceberg analogy mightn't be far from the mark.

My offspring tell me I have a habit of staring at people, and they often chide me for it. I don't do it designedly, but I go into a kind of trance while people-watching and can find myself writing the biographies of strangers who catch me eye for some random reason.

Recently I was stopped at a pedestrian crossing where an older woman, walking with the aid of a stick and carrying a bag of shopping, was slowly making her way from one side of the street to the other. My mental time-machine took her back to when she was a little girl, it had her playing hide and seek or leaping over a skipping rope, light years away from ever being old with a stick, a shopping bag and a shuffle. A hooting fellow-motorist brought me out of my unauthorised biographing of the unsuspecting woman, and I drove on.

What's going on inside under our external frame is a mystery to everyone except ourselves. It can be a mystery to us too. I remember a friend telling me how, at a birthday party for one of her children, she overheard some of the little guests using colourful language. That night, as she tucked the birthday girl into bed, she casually asked her if she ever used bad language, "I know the words, Mammy," she said, "and sometimes I say them, but only inside myself."

There is little doubt but if we gave external expression to some of our internal conversations, we'd certainly lose friends, and might even be arrested. A social filter protects the depths of our iceberg and keeps us from saying what we really think. Euphemisms or double-speak take the sharp edges off our conversation. In my part of the country if someone is 'a bit shook', the diagnosis is bad and they're only a clean shirt from eternity.

If someone admires what you're wearing and tells you, "Not everyone could wear it," what they really mean is, "no-one but yourself would be found in a yoke like that."

Could I be so bold as to say that men are not at all as skilful as women when it comes to the deployment of euphemisms. The day I got married I was very much the picture of a man who enjoyed his food and his tipple, some would say I was carrying a bit of condition. My kinder rural friends would have said I 'got strong' and in racing parlance, I wouldn't have done well on soft ground.

No-one mentioned a word about my appearance until evening came, "when the wine seeped through the veneer," to quote from Paul Brady's great emigrant song, "The Same Old Story". As the vino released the veritas a close friend put his arm around my shoulder and said, "O'Brien you're in powerful condition, you're ready for Henshaw's," Henshaw's being the nearest abattoir to my home place.

In some ways the façade protects us, enabling us to be like an iceberg, maintaining our equilibrium by keeping most of who and what we are hidden from view. This is not a bad strategy, even a cursory glance at "Love Island" paints a disturbing picture of the alternative.

# 25

# Close to the edge

The half-light of our slumbers can be disturbed by a range of classic and recurring nightmares. For a lot of Irish people, the stereotypical one has to do with the Leaving Cert.

In this nightmare the dreamer finds himself or herself sitting in an examination hall as the papers are distributed. When the time is right the invigilator instructs the candidates to turn over their papers and it is then the horror begins. For some, the paper is blank, but for most, a cursory look at the questions tells them they know nothing about the subject or have studied all the wrong things.

In my spare time I occasionally tread the boards as a member of the local amateur drama group. My recurring nightmare finds me walking out on stage on the opening night and realising I know none of my lines. In one particular version of the dream the curtain has gone up when it dawns on me that I haven't been to one rehearsal.

My opposite number in the two-hander is standing there, with a horrified look on his face, waiting for me to deliver the first line. To my relief I see a script taped to a table at the centre of the stage and make a beeline for it, only to find the script open at the last page containing two words – 'THE END'. I wake up in a lather of sweat, never more relieved to find myself in the bed.

Some of my fellow thespians would say I suffer the recurrence of this particular nightmare because it very much reflects the truth – my habit of sailing close to the wind when it comes to learning lines.

I'm inclined to believe that nightmares are a reminder of how close to chaos we are at all times, and how the mere twitch of a muscle or the throw of a word has the potential to land us into all kinds of trouble.

I don't know about you but every now and again I feel tempted to do something completely daft, not because I want to but because I can. I remember as a young fella being bored during the rosary one night and deciding to alleviate the boredom by conducting a scientific experiment. I stuck the poker into the fire and then grabbed hold of it, just to see how it felt. I found out. I presume this is what is meant by devilment, or possession. What possesses us to do certain things? Or perhaps it's just impulse.

In the days before the plague, I made it my business to attend a number of land auctions every year. These can be great spectator events, especially ones that are tightly fought and prolonged. As the bidding progresses the tension is palpable, especially when two bidders remain in the fray and the end comes into sight. Like a pair of gunfighters with a limited supply of ammunition they pace themselves, making every shot count as they take sporadic and careful aim at one another.

The biggest fear of the spectator is that he or she might get caught in the crossfire. As the action reaches its climax the auctioneer will survey the crowd in search of a fresh gunslinger, someone with a pair of loaded six-guns and a Winchester 73 who will carry the fight to a new level. Everyone in the room is afraid to raise an eyebrow, touch a nostril or pull an earlobe in case he or she is identified as the one with the Winchester.

At the same time the devil is moving among the silent and motionless majority looking for anyone who will raise a finger, just for the craic.

With more auctions now happening online I find myself attending a few a week from the increasing discomfort of my own desk. I log on as a spectator and although everything is virtual, the tension can be palpable while the temptation to click the mouse and put in a bid can be overwhelming. The only thing stopping me is the prospect of having to explain to the current consort why our finances are in disarray and why she is now the proud co-owner of 15ac of 'summer grazing' in Shanballymoregurrasheen.

Here in the so-called First World, most of us live such an ordered existence it is easy to forget how close to chaos we are at any given time. It is also frightening to realise that we have extraordinary power over our own lives and could plunge them into turmoil in a second. Any alcoholic who ever fell off the wagon, and got back on, knows all about power, powerlessness, order and chaos.

Our dreams and nightmares give us a taste of these things, in fragile times it is no harm to be aware of them.

# 26

# Through a haze of nostalgia and regret

I was a smoker once, and even though I quit 24 years ago I fear the after-effects might still come back to haunt me. I loved smoking and the rituals around the habit. The best cigarette of the day was enjoyed with a black coffee at around 11 in the morning, it seemed like an appropriate time to light up and let the nicotine course through your system as you got into the stride of the day.

But now, I mostly look back in horror at what I did to myself. I am reminded of it every time I attend a new medical appointment; "Do you smoke?" "No." "Did you ever smoke?" "Yes," and I go on to admit to two decades of tobacco addiction followed by vague answers as to how many a day I smoked. I'm sure I underestimate the volume.

Talking to old smoker friends we sometimes reminisce about the habit, about the brands we preferred and the joys of 'a fag and a pint.' We know the cost and the damage wrought by the addiction, but we put the bad stuff to one side as we wallow in a few moments of nostalgia.

I sometimes wonder, in years to come, when we look back at other aspects of our lives, will we do so through a similar prism of nostalgia and regret? Once the steady march of climate change eventually forces us to alter our habits will we remember, with wicked fondness, the environmentally hazardous things we once enjoyed doing?

If the fates spare me, I can imagine sitting around with my old buddies in 25 years' time, and like old smokers, talking about the things we loved that are no longer loveable.

I was mad about cars, as a young lad I couldn't wait to learn how to drive. I had dream machines I wanted to own, the E-Type jag was the ultimate, or an Aston Martin. If I didn't make a fortune big enough to provide me with marques of that stature, I would have been content with a Triumph Stag, an MG or a Triumph Spitfire. We were very Anglophile in our motoring tastes in those days, aside from the Volkswagen Beetle and the Porsche, 'foreign cars' weren't rated.

In terms of achievable vehicles, the Ford Capri was much admired along with the souped-up Hillman Avenger and, of course, the cheeky Mini Cooper S.

We loved to drive. Weekends were spent on the go. It was no bother to travel the length and breadth of the country on bad roads in bad cars. When times turned good, we quickly developed a fondness for the luxurious European models and their far eastern counterparts. And as the depths of the environmental crisis hit home, we had embraced the wasteful SUV.

Yes indeed, in moments of wry reminiscence, we will recall how we loved our fossil fuel carriages, the purr of their engines, the smell of hot oil and the rasp of a rusty exhaust pipe. With the perspective of hindsight, we will ask ourselves what we thought we were at, pumping tons bad stuff into the atmosphere with no concern for tomorrow.

And we will shake our heads when we recall crowded airports and millions of planes traversing the globe for little reason, pouring megatons of $CO_2$ into the upper echelons of the elements for the sake of a suntan or a few pints. We will remember getting to Prague for €2.99 and Rome for a tenner, not to mention that weekend in New York for the January sales where we went everywhere by stretch limo. "It was good while it lasted," someone will say, "but we've paid for it since."

As farmers look out across land with a wild head on it they will remember the days when it was like a lawn, with not a weed, bush or hedge to be seen.

We will shake our heads at the memory of the sheets of plastic that wrapped carrots, parsnips, broccoli, beer, bread and even dogfood. We will remember how handy it was and wonder where it is all gone and what it's doing to us now.

Yes, we will look back like old smokers, who loved the habit until the damage became too obvious to ignore.

# 27

# Onboarding, whatever happened to hiring?

It's the height of summer, and while there's a general preoccupation with soaring temperatures and lower stress levels, the jobs market isn't taking a holiday. A lively hunt for recruits is under way out there.

I hear stories of young people being offered two or three positions as companies poach employees from one another on the basis of a glance at a CV and a quick phone chat. Entry level jobs appear to be coming along faster than there are people to fill them, I have seen some evidence of this under my own roof.

Over the past few weeks, as the first of our offspring engages with the world of Human Resources (HR), I've become a dab hand at the lingo, as you will have seen from my casual use of the term 'entry level.' And there's a new word for hiring – it's the verb to 'onboard' – "we are onboarding new team members to share our journey with us." This latest addition to the language describes the process of employing and integrating recruits into a company or organisation. I presume the opposite is 'overboarding', but I doubt we will hear corporate press releases using that word anytime soon. They'll stick to 'downsizing'.

Onboarding is an amalgam of noun, adverb and verb. In my own corner of the country, they'd call it a 'mixum-gatherum' of a thing. In that haven of erudition that cradled me we latinise our language and lionise our hurlers (with good reason). It's a place where the classics and classical references pepper the most mundane of conversations. There were, and are, Latinate words for all manner of things. For instance, the cure for a poor sexual appetite was known as a 'coaxiorum'. Like Charlie Haughey's contraceptives, it was available only to married people and dispensed by someone who knew her potions from her poisons.

A classical subculture bubbled away under every day. I remember a travelling insurance man recounting to my father and mother the details of a post prandial conversation in a farm kitchen between the woman of the house and a local agricultural contractor. The man had just 'knocked' a field of hay and was having the dinner before knocking any more.

A renowned lover of his grub, he peeled, sliced, buttered and salted his way through a half stone of spuds, a fletch of bacon and at least one head of cabbage. This was followed by a bowl of ambrosia rice with a dollop of strawberry jam sitting like a ruby in the middle of it. To complete the repast, he was served a cup of strong tea and a 'wadge' of buttered porter cake. As he followed the last crumbs of the cake around the plate, the woman bustled about, attending to her many duties and probably wondering if the hay-knocker was ever going to take his legs out from under her table.

"What you need, Missus," he opined, "is a general factotum."

"Indeed, I do," she replied, "and I'd need to hold on to him in saecula, saeculorum. Now, off with you, the meadow won't knock itself." I'm not sure the woman was glad she 'onboarded' that particular contractor but there was great pleasure in feeding him.

Saving hay and silage provides a steady stream of 'entry level' jobs for rural young lads, and has done so for decades. It is often the first taste of paid work many a male rural youngster gets. As for onboarding, there isn't much of a process involved. I once witnessed a silage lad's induction, and it took all of 30 seconds. The employer pointed the new recruit in the direction of the tractor he was to drive and said,

"Let me warn you, there's bad brakes in that thing,"

"So, how am I supposed to stop it?" the wide-eyed neophyte asked.

"Close it down, stand on it and pray to St Jude the hoor of a thing will stop."

While the onboarding or induction might have been spartan, the performance monitoring and appraisal system was even more basic. There were three key performance indicators; "did you turn up, did you drive like hell, and did you avoid destruction?"

Of course, spartan onboarding isn't the preserve of agricultural contractors. In years gone by many a young priest found himself dispatched to his first appointment with little induction or introduction.

In one case a young man arrived at an isolated parochial house to take up his duties. The Canon's housekeeper showed him into the parlour where his reverence was reading the newspaper. Without looking up the older clergyman asked, "Who are you?"

"I'm your new curate, Canon."

"And who sent you?"

"The bishop."

"Huh," grunted the well-seasoned Canon, "doesn't he know there's nothin' to be done here and I'm already doin' that."

Maybe onboarding isn't such a bad idea, but it's still a terrible word.

# 28

# August, I dread you

The title of Edna O'Brien's fourth novel tells us that 'August is a wicked month' – there's a lot of truth in it.

Much of the population of the northern hemisphere takes holidays in August, making it a frustrating time for anyone dealing with officialdom, there's hardly a body left to answer a phone or a send an email. It's a time when the world can be caught napping and all manner of skulduggery happens.

For instance, the beginnings of the Berlin Wall emerged between August 13 and 15, 1961. While the West was on holidays, East German soldiers laid down 50km of barbed wire across the city and began the process of cutting the Russian sector off from the rest. By the time the relaxing world leaders came to grips with the situation the barbed wire had turned into concrete.

When Sadaam Hussein decided to invade Kuwait, he did it in August, 1990. I remember I was on the Dingle Peninsula when the news broke and happened to run into a good friend of mine on the street with a paper under his arm. I asked him what was big in the news and he told me that Kuwait was no more, "Ta sé imithe." Not that I could have done much about it. Many of the people who could have done something were away from their desks, sitting on sunlounges sipping cocktails, delighted to get a break from the affairs of state.

In Paris in the early hours of the morning of August 10, 1792, a rampage of revolutionaries invaded the Royal Palace at the Tuileries causing King Louis and his family to flee and take refuge in the National Assembly. That was the beginning of the end for the French monarchy. It happened in August, a month when nothing is supposed to happen in Paris.

The timetable for the beginning of the First World war would make one very wary of the month. On August 1, 1914, Germany declared war on Russia, on August 3, Germany declared war on France, on

August 4, Britain declared war on Germany and on August 6 Austria declared war on Russia. That was some start to the annual break.

All kinds of people with all manner of ill intent take advantage of this lull in life when the engine is idling, when even those at the wheel feel entitled to nod off. On August 21, 1911, an Italian handyman, Vincenzo Perrugia was working at the Louvre decided it was an opportune time to help himself to Da Vinci's *Mona Lisa*. He was eventually nabbed and got seven months for his trouble.

I don't really associate holidays with August. Traditionally the building industry shut down for the first two weeks of the month, but life on the land continued very much as normal. Except, of course, for the international showjumping from the RDS – we always took a break to watch the preliminary rounds on telly and certainly parked the tractors and the pitchforks for the final of the Aga Khan Cup.

We didn't own a horse and could just about tell a piebald from a Clydesdale, but, after a week of immersion in the events broadcast from the RDS, we became experts in all things equestrian. We knew the horses and riders well. Eddie Macken and Carroll's Boomerang were heroes and the irreverent Yorkshire horseman, Harvey Smith, was Ireland's favourite Englishman until Jack Charlton came along. But then there was that exotic Italian army officer in his fantastic uniform, Captain Raimondo D'Inzeo. The Irish commentators loved rolling their tongues around every syllable of his name, "And…, representing Italy, we have Captain Rrrraymondooh D'Inzeooooh.

As an aside, D'Inzeo was an Olympian. He and his older brother Piero were the first athletes to represent their country in eight consecutive Olympics, from 1948 to 1976. While we're talking Olympics, could I mention that the Chef d'Equipe of the current Irish Olympic show jumping team, Michael Blake, hails from my neighbouring parish of Tuamgraney and is a nephew of the aforementioned Edna O'Brien.

I digress, let me go back to August and its wicked capacity for surprise. I remember during one particular Aga Khan Cup, as we watched an unfortunate Irish team crash through every wall, knock every pole and splash around in the water jump, our cows took advantage of our distraction and broke out. By the time we went to bring them in for milking, they had eaten their way through four paddocks. Like Sadaam Hussein and Vincenzo Perrugia, they decided August was a good month for smashing borders and engaging in thievery.

As we strolled them towards the milking parlour my brother suggested that, given the way they had soared over fences and avoided obstacles on their breakout, we should select four of the best of them to represent Ireland in next year's Aga Khan Cup.

August is a quare month.

# 29

# Pulling like a dog

I haven't seen much of the Olympic games but the bits I have seen are remarkable. Even a glimpse at the superhuman efforts the athletes put in to compete at this level would bring you to the edge of wonder.

In the less than the ten seconds it takes to complete an Olympic 100m dash you can witness perfection, disaster, ecstasy, and heartbreak. Years of rigorous preparation can be crowned with achievement or wiped out in the blink of an eye. The physical, psychological, and emotional strength it takes to be an Olympian surely takes these people out of the realm of the ordinary and ranks them among the extraordinary.

We were chatting about it around our table recently and agreed that being an Olympian must be an enormous asset on a CV. It would surely guarantee any job applicant a place on an interview shortlist and a real shot at the job – if the qualifications are in the least bit relevant. The discipline, dedication, attention to detail and resilience it takes to reach the Olympics would be welcome on any team.

But even when one gets to the Olympics, winning a medal can be as far away as ever. The numbers give a sense of the enormity of the challenge. In the Tokyo Olympics over 11,000 athletes from 206 nations across 33 sports competed for 339 medals.

Once the athletes are finished in Tokyo, with or without medals, they begin to focus on the next competition; the European Championships or the Olympics in Paris in 2024. Their success or lack of it is put to one side as they lift their eyes to the next horizon.

The number of human beings that choose to stretch themselves to this extent is rare. Perhaps astronauts can be numbered among them, or lone sailors who try to circumnavigate the globe, climbers of Everest, or those who volunteer to join special forces. While all are willing to push themselves to the limit of human endurance, for most there will be no medal at the end and for some the result will be oblivion. Yet they choose to do it.

In the more mundane world, there are people who find themselves in profoundly challenging situations that are not of their choosing. For many, every day can be a marathon that takes them to the heights and depths, physically, emotionally, and psychologically. Added to that can be the exasperation of dealing with a cumbersome and heedless bureaucracy, where agencies that are meant to help can often be a source of agony and frustration. There are days, I'm sure, when the well of love is almost dry and the arid reserves of duty just have to do.

The Olympics model the challenges of being human. In a few short weeks they take us, again and again, to the extremes of exhilaration and despair. They show us how a lifetime's work can be burned to a shred by a slight miscalculation. Yet, the athlete with her lower lip held quivering between her teeth, or the one with bitter tears flooding down his face will be in the gym, or the pool, or on the track the following day, believing again. When the well of talent is running dry the arid reserves of persistence will have to suffice.

While the Olympics do agony, ecstasy and loss, they don't do despair. They do resilience and perspective. I remember Sonia O'Sullivan's father being interviewed at the Atlanta Olympics shortly after Sonia had to exit the 5,000 metres final due to a tummy bug. The breathless interviewer was trying to quantify the loss when Mr O'Sullivan calmed him down with a bit of perspective, "Listen," he said, "there's no one dead."

The Olympics present us with a veritable caricature of human capability. They stretch the participants in all directions. As spectators we get a glimpse of what can happen when life is thrown at people in all its extremities, and we learn that while joy can be unconfined, disappointment doesn't have to become despair.

Like our Olympic rowers, there are days when the oars hardly crack the water, so sweet are the strokes that propel us along, and there are days when we just have to pull like a dog.

# 30

# The Bard of Passage West

I had a strange dream last week. I dreamed I was at an open-air concert in the carpark of one of the local churches. There are two houses of worship in this little lakeside community, one is down by the main road and the other is in the hills, a beautiful pre-Emancipation cruciform building high above Lough Derg.

Anyway, I dreamed my neighbours and friends were sitting on chairs around the carpark in bunches of three or four. Everyone was dressed for a damp Irish evening. A stage had been set up in a corner of the yard, while the old church formed a magnificent background bathed in a soft flood of multicoloured light.

Suddenly the stage lights came on, catching the sparkling mist that swirled around the gathering. Harpist Niamh O'Brien and guitarist Steve Ryan appeared on stage. Her ethereal, feather-delicate voice and the sweetness of her harping wafted over the audience, down the hillside and out over Lough Derg. It felt great to be there.

In dreams, no one questions the unusual and so no-one questioned why we were sitting out of doors, under the elements while the church beside us stood empty.

Then, out of the night, like Merlin rising from the lake, John Spillane, the Bard of Passage West, materialised at the microphone singing his haunting tribute to the Banner, *Under the Old Clare Moon*.

The tunes took over, and in the oilskinned and huddled crowd we sang along with songs like *Oró, 'Sé Do Bheatha 'Bhaile* and lost ourselves in the gentle quirkiness of Spillane's canon of song.

I woke to discover it wasn't a dream at all – what seemed unreal had actually happened. On Saturday evening, August 7, John Spillane performed in the carpark of St Marys Church at the Gap of Ogonnolloe. If you don't believe me, look it up on Google or Facebook or any other such window to the world.

The idea for the event came about when a group of locals decided to celebrate the first stirrings of post-pandemic life with a concert.

Thanks to funding from the Department of Tourism, Arts, Culture, the Gaeltacht, Sport & Media and from the Arts Office at Clare Co Council, they were able to bring Spillane all the way from Cork and ensure that the best of sound, light and staging was available. A local man, Ger Kilkenny, who makes his bread and butter from this sort of thing, was only too delighted to gather his crew and wheel out his lights, mics, amps and speakers from the silent storerooms that held them since March 2020.

There was a lovely touch of resurrection about the gig. The wonder of it was brought home to us when Niamh, opening proceedings, explained it was her first gig in eighteen months. From then on, the weather didn't matter – it was good to be there. Even though the sky threatened and sometimes the mist swept thickly across our coats and hats the music lifted us out of ourselves – with the help of a few nips from bottle, flask and naggin.

It was a night to savour and remember, a night to think of all the musicians, singers and artists consigned to the shadows by the plague. These kept the faith and explored other ways and other platforms to give expression to their work. They found audiences wherever they could and performed when there was little to be got for it.

I'm thinking of people like Eimer Dunne, a singer and musician from Laois whose eternal optimism and hard work will surely be rewarded when the half-light of these days gives way to a full dawn. I'm thinking of the two-piece, three-piece and eight-piece bands that played for every kind of community and family function and who, for months on end, have been unable earn a living doing what they love doing. And of course, there are those who filled the halls on the dancing and country music circuit and can't wait to get back. Not to mention the actors, comedians and stage crews who have been missing the lives they once had. They want to be back creating, in a world fuelled by the buzz of an audience.

Sitting in the carpark on that August night it was indeed like a dream; the scenario made no sense; rows of hooded heads sitting in the mist and the half-light with smiles on their faces and joy in their eyes.

Towards the end of the night, John Spillane took us away with him into the spellbinding hope of his trademark song, *The Dance of the Cherry Trees*. In it he describes how, every April, year in and year out, the cherry trees dress outrageously to sing and congratulate the world on another year of life, "Well done everyone, well done."

# 31

# Hard facts and the destruction of fiction

One night, a few years ago, I went to meet a friend in a pub I had never been to. As soon as I opened the door the barman extended his right arm, pointed his finger at me and asked, "Patsy Cline, car crash or plane crash?" I looked behind to see who he was talking to, but I was the only person at the door. Four men perched on high stools along the counter stared at me, waiting for an answer to the question. I thought it was a rite of passage to gain entry.

The barman resolved my puzzlement when he explained the topic of conversation at the counter before I arrived was the tragic deaths of famous musicians and singers. The participants had established how Buddy Holly, Jim Reeves, Jim Croce and a few others had met their ends, but were stuck on how poor Patsy Cline died. They hoped I might have the answer. I admitted my ignorance on the matter, called for a pint and waited for my friend.

The conversation continued and all kinds of theories were put forward as to why so many celebrities died in car and air accidents. The speculating and theorising lasted for at least another hour, long after my friend arrived.

I remember another encounter with the universal and all-embracing nature of pub conversation. At 11 o clock one morning, having arrived early for an appointment in a small town in the West, I passed the spare time in a licensed premises among pre-noon drinkers. I ordered a mug of coffee and as I grimaced my way through its thin and scalded contents the scintillating conversation at the counter more than compensated for what I was trying to swallow.

The topic was informed by the television, suspended from the ceiling over the counter and tuned to a news channel. It must have been the month of June because the pictures on the screen featured footage from the Normandy invasion of 1944 and live coverage from commemoration ceremonies at the graveyards near the beaches.

"Do you know," said a customer propped up against the wall at the end of the counter, "that the Irish played a fierce important part in that invasion."

"How could we," asked his neighbour, "weren't we neutral?"

"Ah, but we were neutral on one side," said the expert. "We were of massive help in three ways. Firstly, a woman working in a post office in west Mayo gave General Eisenhower the clearance to go ahead when she sent him a forecast for good weather. Secondly, hundreds of Irish men went ashore with the allied armies. And, thirdly, Irish mountain goats were used to clear the minefields."

"Is that a fact?" asked another, "the poor auld goats must have been killed in their droves."

"They were not indeed," replied the expert, "hardly one of them was lost."

"Erra how did they manage that?" a sceptic at the other end of the counter demanded to know.

"I'll tell you. These mountain goats were trained to smell out explosives buried under the ground. What's more, as soon as they'd stand on the buttons that triggered the devices they'd leap into the air and would be gone before the things exploded. Those goats got Victoria Crosses, Purple Hearts and all kinds of decorations. Look it up."

The man finished with such authority and threw down the challenge to 'look it up' with such confidence that no one dared question him. Even the sceptic nodded and returned to the dark depths of his morning pint.

Alas, these conversations can never happen nowadays. The wild theories and tall tales told by the men of the 'counter culture' are killed at birth by the search engines at the beck and call of every mobile phone carried in almost every hand in the land. They give immediate access to the Smithsonian, the Imperial War Museum and every other authoritative source on the planet. Any story you tell can be checked out immediately as the tyranny of fact smothers the wild wonder of speculation.

Of course, there is the 'dark web' and a myriad of sinister rabbit holes down which one can go to prove or embrace any theory. But, in general, most things can be checked out by scrolling down a screen.

Pub counters and pub conversations have lost much of their wonder and the unpredictable contours of speculative discourse have given way to the steel and unyielding symmetry of hard fact. As we prepare for the full return of the 'wet pub' is it time to contemplate the 'fact-free pub', where wild speculation is encouraged, wi-fi is banned and the very utterance of the word 'Google' will get one barred?

By the way, poor Patsy Cline died in a plane crash, and there is no mention of Irish goats in action on the beaches of Normandy in 1944. I looked it up on you-know-where.

# 32

# Gathering no moss

As I sat down to write this piece the news broke that veteran Rolling Stones drummer, Charlie Watts, had died at 80. He had been drumming with the band since 1963 – fifty-eight years in all.

My goodness is it really fifty-eight years since 1963, when the world felt like one long Saturday afternoon, where the air smelled of hairspray, aftershave and Brylcreem, where cars were innocent things, adorned in walnut and leather and sparkling all over with chrome?

In those days, time passed in hours and minutes, now it feels as if it is whizzing by in epochs. Where does it go?

Charlie Watts' departure to the beat of the eternal drum certainly put me in mind of the fleeting feet of time. It caused me to remember, of all things, the first manure spreader we had at home on the farm. That might seem like a random association of ideas, but with a memory bank that's nearly full, I make no apology if incident, image, recall and reflection run randomly into one another.

Anyway, the first artificial manure spreader we had was made up of two conical containers sitting on a wheeled frame. Manure pellets from the containers fell on to spinning plates fitted with fins and driven by a cog and groove mechanism powered by the wheels. The spreader was attached to the tractor when working on the land and when travelling between jobs it was pulled behind a trailer carrying the manure.

As was the custom with a lot of farm machinery the spreader was shared among a number of farmers. One day my uncle came to collect it, and of course was invited into the house for a cup of tea. No one left the premises without tay. He parked the tractor with the attached trailer and spreader on an incline leading out our gate and on to the public road. More than likely the starter or the battery weren't doing their job, a common problem, so it was left on the incline ready for a 'hill start'.

While the adults were inside having the tea, I availed of the opportunity to conduct an experiment. I reckoned that if the wheels could turn the spreading plates, the spreading plates should be able to turn the wheels. To test my theory, I grabbed hold of a fin on one of the plates and pulled with all my might. To my surprise, not only did the wheels of the spreader start to move, so did those on the trailer and, horror of horrors, the tractor wheels followed suit.

Before I knew it, all three pieces of machinery were heading for the gate and gathering speed as they went. I tried in vain to hold them back by hanging on to the spreader, but my boots could get no grip in the gravel. I was left sitting on my backside watching the components of my experiment hurtling to disaster. I can still feel the panic. To my great relief, as the tractor reached the gate the trailer jack-knifed and the towbar jammed itself between the ridges of the rear tractor tyre bringing the whole menagerie to a halt. I sat on the ground, completely relieved that tragedy had been avoided and experienced a rare moment of bliss. I soon picked myself off the ground and disappeared down the fields to escape the public inquiry that was sure to follow.

The same panic and the accompanying sense that things are out of control can grip me at the strangest of times and in the oddest places. The death of someone like Charlie Watts, a man I didn't know, can jolt me into recognising the broad span of my days and the number of milestones I have passed. It's like falling asleep on a bus leaving Dublin and waking up in Annacotty.

I suppose that's what mindfulness is about, being conscious of the present, of the moment you are in right now and not wishing it was any other time. We get tasters of that, fleeting senses of what it is to be absolutely present to the now. I had that sense after Limerick's recent hurling triumph in Croke Park. As the Cranberries' *Dreams* pulsated through the sea of green swaying around the stadium, there was no other place I wanted to be, no other time I wanted it to be in and there was no other feeling I wanted to have. It was pure bliss.

Every now and again the towbar gets stuck in the back wheel, the fleeting becomes slow motion and a space opens up where you can breathe deeply and luxuriate in the eternal wealth of the moment.

# 33

# The joys of a temperamental French motor

Among the drawbacks of working from home is the relative isolation. It is safe, secure and predictable but the boundaries of the world can contract and expectations can become sanitised – same stuff different day.

Farmers are accustomed to the life of the lone operator and are well used to spending most of their days in their own company. They are probably more isolated now than they ever were. Increased mechanisation means that they don't need to call in extra help too often.

In times gone by the trip to the creamery was an opportunity to go beyond the gate. On wet days farmers liked nothing more than spending a few hours in the forge. When our local forge closed my father would pass many a wet afternoon in the workshop of a man who made gates and feeding troughs and straightened warped machinery parts.

It is good to have an excuse to get out, even if it's only to cross-pollinate the content of one's conversation. We have a diesel car that provides me with such an excuse on a regular basis. It has more mileage on the clock than the International Space Station and hardly a month goes by but it needs a visit to the garage. Just when you think all its moving parts are going like a mouse's heart some red or orange light flashes to warn you of an impending crisis under the bonnet.

The car is French and something of a drama queen as it struggles to embrace the onset of late middle age. At the first sign of a problem the dash will light up like the control room in a melting nuclear power plant. A bright red warning will order you to STOP – ENGINE FAILURE HAZARD. The first time it happened I nearly drove into the lake thinking I needed to cool down the central core before the thing exploded under me.

Over time I've learned not to take the warnings too seriously. A bit of coaxing, patience and automotive TLC goes a long way towards humouring the machine and preventing it from taking itself too seriously. I imagine if it was a human, it would wear a feather boa, carry a foot-long cigarette holder and wheeze its way through calling everyone 'dawling.'

Its foibles regularly get me out of the house and down to the garage where a father and son team have developed an intimate knowledge of the innards of this Gallic machine. Sometimes major surgery is required, like the replacing of a clutch or colonic irrigation of the diesel particulate filter (the DPF to those of us familiar with these things). At other times it's just the onboard computer acting up, suggesting admission for an automotive spa day. After a filter change, an oil replenishment and a coolant top-up it drives home purring like a pampered Parisian cat.

On the days I sign it in for its therapies, I retire to the local Italian café where there is always someone more interesting than myself to talk to. I get to use my thin spattering of Italian while chatting with the genial host and, as I sip my espresso, I imagine I'm back in the Piazza Barberini with forty years shaved off the speedometer and the promise of a Roman night stretching out before my supple young limbs.

As a family we are not totally dependent on the French voiture. We also have an electric car, an ideal vehicle for living in a bubble. It is completely predictable and doesn't afford many moments of unplanned encounter. In fact, it is too perfect, nothing ever goes wrong, the absence of an internal combustion engine means it doesn't even backfire occasionally to break the monotony.

The only time it provides an opportunity for a bit of diversion is when you have to stop at a charging point to top up. Here conversations between the passing EV owners inevitably revolve around how long it takes yours to charge and how long the charge will last. An untrained ear eavesdropping on such chats would be forgiven for thinking the participants are comparing notes on the duration and intensity of their lovemaking. I suppose it provides a welcome distraction from the predictability of the perfect world.

The history of civilisation is, in many ways, the story of the human reach for perfection, the search to create an ideal world where angst, pain and uncertainty are no more – where there's a vaccine, a therapy and a piece of legislation to cover every eventuality. It is interesting to note that one of the fastest growing sectors in the area of management is risk management.

But it's the imperfections that make life interesting. They drive us into one another's company and one another's arms. To paraphrase the great Leonard Cohen, it's the cracks that let the light in. The faults and foibles of my middle-aged French motor get me out of the house. They have introduced me to an obliging and competent family of mechanics and give me the excuse to go for coffee on a weekday afternoon where I can babble Italian and dream of balmy Roman evenings that had a great welcome for the youth of me.

# 34

# Living the dream

Some time ago I was travelling with an auctioneer to walk a farm of land. We stopped at temporary traffic lights set up at road works on a relatively quiet country road. We were the third vehicle back from the lights and the last in the queue. It was a dull wet day, the kind that wouldn't lift the spirits. Just beyond the light a man in yellow overalls and a hard hat was waist-deep in a hole shovelling out stone and mud by the dripping shovel full.

Looking at him from the comfort of the car I remarked to my host, "That's some tough job on a day like this."

"What job?" he asked

"What the lad is at in the hole is at," I replied.

'Oh I know the fella," he said, "a gas man. These conditions don't bother him."

As we drove past after the light turned green my host let down the passenger window and shouted, "Good man yourself Mick, you're hard at it."

"Oh livin' the dream," he shouted back, "livin' the dream, what else would I be at?"

"Fair dues to him," I said, "the power of positive thinking."

"It's more than that," my auctioneer friend said, "he is one happy man. He worked for years in the States and England, all he wanted to do was come home, and he did. He bought a house on 25ac where he keeps a few cattle. With the farm and his council job he has all he wants. As far as he's concerned, he is definitely livin' the dream."

Thankfully there are as many definitions of living the dream as there are people with dreams. I remember talking to a farmer friend of mine during the depths of the recent recession. He was in bother. A few investments he had made during the boom had become a necklace of millstones around him. Every day the postman and the phone brought nothing but trouble, letter after letter and call after call reminded him of the chronic nature of his finances.

I'd meet him occasionally and we'd sit on a wall or lean against the wheel of a tractor chatting about things in general and about his predicament in particular. One day I suggested that he should consider selling a portion of an out-farm.

"Why would I do that?" he asked

"It would take some of the pressure off and reduce your stress levels."

"Listen," he said, "I enjoy the stress, it keeps me keen. I'd miss it if it was gone."

I gave up worrying about him after that. There is no doubt, but one person's pain is another's pleasure.

The release of the CAO offers last week saw a lot of young people take crucial steps on the road to living the dream. While some landed on their feet others found their expectations dashed and all their hard work seemingly disregarded by a system that can be capricious and cruel.

All attempts to tweak the process seem to make it worse, and why wouldn't they? The thing is fundamentally flawed. For a start it is one dimensional in its assessment of the skills and intelligences of those caught up in it. Secondly, in its attempts to standardise human achievement it inevitably creates victims and victors.

Nearly 30 years have passed since Harvard psychologist Howard Gardner published *Frames of Mind,* a book outlining his theory of multiple intelligences. He based the theory on his work with a range of people including children of average intelligence and ability, gifted children and brain-damaged adults.

Arising from his studies he argued that there are many different intelligences and multiple ways of thinking and learning. He identified eight distinct types that include interpersonal intelligence, intrapersonal intelligence, kinesthetic intelligence (associated with sports, movement, dance), musical intelligence, naturalistic intelligence, visual-spatial intelligence (builders, tradespeople, crafts people, creators), linguistic-verbal intelligence and mathematical intelligence.

It appears to me that our entire education system is only concerned with the last two and if you don't fit in you are left out. Achievement in our system has more to do with navigation, shoe-horning, grinning and bearing than with growing and blossoming .

It would seem to me that a core function of the education system is to guide and nurture young people as they search for the dawn of the dream that inspires them. And it shouldn't matter where this dream is to be realised – in the board room, the sports ground, the stage, or in a hole at the side of the road where you can dig to your hearts content as you plan what you will do next with your few acres.

# 35

# A meditative disaster

I've been quite stressed of late. I took on a project last year that has had a long and relatively pleasant gestation, but as it's due date looms the birth is proving difficult. The contractions have been going on for more than a month now and show no signs of abating. There is equally no sign the progeny is ready to leave the safety of the huge and burgeoning folder forming a womb in the abdominal depths of my computer.

The current consort, weary of my grumbling and grousing, has put down an ultimatum: either I get myself the writer's equivalent of a C-section or I take myself off to a scribbler's hermitage where I can groan, moan and howl at the moon all I like. Maybe something more local might be in order.

Normally at this time of year people take on projects. The summer is over, and many are cracking their knuckles eager to get doing stuff to fill the long evenings. Some will head out to the local hall, hotel or hostelry with sandals on and their yoga mats under their oxters. There, the soothing voice of the teacher wafting over them with concise instructions will help them summon the body's healing power allowing its balm to course through tension-tightened joints that creak at every move.

I tried yoga once and, while it was nice, I felt it did nothing for me that a good walk wouldn't do. I don't think I'll be heading to an ashram at the foot of the Himalayas in sandals and a loincloth anytime soon. Nevertheless, the notion of yoga sounds tempting to anyone with a body that has turned into a board.

Perhaps Pilates, a far-out German cousin of yoga, might be the job? Its regime of gentle exercise is highly recommended by people familiar with the architecture of the body. In my own neighbourhood a group of local men from all walks of life attend a weekly session in the back room of a local hostelry. A friend has invited me to take it up, but I have hummed and hawed about the notion. In case I might be worried that it is not 'a man's thing' I am assured by practitioners that real men do Pilates. As someone who struggles with what exactly a real man is, this reassurance is kind of lost on me.

Other people have suggested meditation, but I've been trying to meditate for years. I've come to the conclusion that it doesn't suit me. You see, I hail from a long line of inveterate daydreamers who can drift off into another world anytime, anyplace, and anywhere. At weddings, wakes, hurling matches or horror movies we can find another world to get lost in. When it comes to meditation our family is genetically programmed to resist it.

I have tried various versions of the discipline, but as soon as the incense is smouldering, and I close my eyes the imagination takes off like a balloon on a breezy day. And it won't necessarily land in any exotic spot or be inspired by any philosophical profundity. Out of nowhere I'll remember that one of the tyres on the car is bald. Next, I'm wondering if I should replace it on its own, or maybe I should get two new tyres for the front and use one of the existing tyres as a spare. Then I'll remember there is no such thing as a spare wheel these days, there's an emergency wheel. At that realisation I'll take to surmising how much money the car manufacturers are saving by not supplying spare wheels. Then I might go off on a side trip, exploring the possibility of buying an actual wheel to replace the emergency wheel but, the question is, would a real wheel fit in the compartment under the boot where the emergency wheel is kept? What a major existential conundrum.

By the time the incense has burned itself to a long piece of ash, all I'll have managed to do is get lost in a loop of uselessness inspired by a bald tyre.

On another day an attempt at meditation might find me off again in my own world rewriting the narrative of the battle of Aughrim or wondering would we all be speaking Spanish if the Armada had succeeded in breaking Elizabeth's England. I'm a meditative disaster.

Once my current project has left the birthing chamber, maybe I should keep the options for the long evenings simple – a good walk, an odd pint and a decent book. Perhaps it's no harm to leave the dreaming to the dark of night, the yoga to the loose of limb and the meditation to the gurus.

# 36

# Risk and compliance behind a box hedge

My phone beeped the other day, as it often does. This time it alerted me to a group message sent to the members of an organisation in which I'm involved, asking if it's time to start meeting again. I must admit I broke out in a bit of a sweat. I've grown accustomed to not going to meetings, to having nothing beyond the demands of the day job and the family to contend with.

I'm sure I'm not the only one. I notice the attendance at the Balmoral Show was well down on pre pandemic numbers. I had expected our northern cousins to come out in force for the occasion. Talking to friends and neighbours they speak of a nervousness at the prospect of going back to the way things were. It is remarkable how quickly we become creatures of habit. It doesn't take too much to muffle the adventurous spirit in a world where erring on the side of caution predominates.

The last eighteen months has not been good for the adventurous among us. We no longer hear about people who are taking off to circumnavigate the world on a bicycle or going to live in a yurt in Mongolia or with the Bedouins in North Africa. We have become very much confined to our own backyard, hemmed in by fear. The tragedy is, we're getting used to it.

I remember reading that when the Birmingham Six were released after 16 years in prison, one thing it took them ages to become accustomed to was opening doors for themselves. For more than a decade and a half they had to stand back while others with bunches of keys did it for them. For a long time after their ordeal, they would find themselves standing at doors, waiting, before it dawned on them they could reach out and turn the handle for themselves.

This past year and a half has not just been a time of confinement of the body, it has also been a time of confinement of the spirit, when the energy that drives our evolution went into suspended animation. I wonder if there is a danger that, just as the virus mutates and changes, will we also mutate into something safer and more cautious.

When the children were younger, every year we went on holidays to France. We had a big tank of a campervan that took us from Normandy to the Alps and even to the French Riviera. The campsites were fascinating places for a people-watcher and a nosey parker like me. Many of our camping neighbours were a study. Although they had opted to spend their holidays living in a campsite many of them sought to bring all the comforts of home with them. These included their security measures and the things that safeguarded their privacy, like zero eye-contact and faux box hedges they laid down to mark the perimeter of their territory.

When the current consort would catch me studying the set-up of our neighbours' box-hedged universes she would tell me to mind my own business, "They'd be better off if they had stayed at home," I'd say, "they're completely stressed out trying to replicate it."

I'm afraid the pandemic experience might box us into the vain pursuit of a completely risk-free way of life, where every corner of our existence must be sanitised. Risk is an essential element of being human; it moves us on, it makes us innovate, it prevents stagnation. Risk is a vital ingredient in the formation of relationships. It can also break them, and it is certainly needed to heal them.

Over the last few months, I have been involved in compiling a history of our local credit union. It is celebrating its 50th anniversary this year having opened its doors in 1971 after a group of volunteers got together to found it. They gathered people's money to create a fund from which local people could borrow when they needed to. They took the risk of asking their neighbours for money, the neighbours took the risk of giving it and the board took the further risk of lending it to members of the community. It was used to buy everything from sewing machines to tractors, from a few cattle to a hat for a wedding or the honeymoon in Majorca.

Over the course of 50 years this small local credit union has amassed as asset base in excess of €33m. Over €107m has passed in and out of its loan book transforming a lot of lives along the way. Soon after the crash of 2008 the credit unions nationally got a new master, the Central Bank. This new master has two preoccupations, risk management and compliance, little else seems to matter. Aren't the credit union members lucky the risk takers had their job done before the Central Bank arrived with its box hedge?

Now, I'd better smarten myself, I have a meeting to go to.

# 37

## To the empress of beverages

I drank my first cup of coffee during a late-night and illicit visit to the kitchen in the college where I was boarded. My friend and companion on the mission was a lad from the far west who believed rules and regulations were made to be flouted. He was in search of coffee, which he found on one of the shelves in the shape of a jar of Maxwell House. Turning his attention to the AGA cooker he lifted the lid on one of rings and moved the giant kettle into place.

"This will be boiled in a minute, O'Brien. Will I make you a coffee?"

"I've never tasted the stuff," I answered, "I'm not sure I'd like it."

"Well, it's about time you tried it," he said, "I can't let you out into the world without having tasted coffee, they'll say you've no class. Sit down there and I'll make you one."

He treated the kitchen like it was his own, "Do you take sugar in tea?" he asked, "I do," I replied, "Then you'll take sugar in coffee." He handed me my cup of the steaming liquid, the first of about 50,000 I've drunk since.

I began to gulp it down, afraid we might be nabbed by a prowling dean. However, my friend settled himself at the end of the kitchen table ready to enjoy his brew at a leisurely pace.

"Come on," I said, "drink up and let's go, we'll be caught."

"What's your rush," he asked, "they'll hardly throw us out now, we're in Leaving Cert."

With that he took out a packet of cigarettes and a lighter. This was taking things to a new level entirely – smoking was absolutely forbidden. To be found out of bounds in the kitchen was one thing but to be found out of bounds, drinking staff coffee and smoking cigarettes was like driving up to a Garda checkpoint with a bottle of beer in your hand and a cannabis plant on your lap.

"Settle down O'Brien," he said, "you can't have coffee without a fag, they're the perfect combination." I should add that a few months previously the same friend bought me my first drink, the beginning of another life-long relationship. He had me well ready for the world by the time we left our Brideshead of the south.

As the years have gone by coffee has developed a culture of its own wrapping an aura of sophistication around itself. White-shirted baristas are to be found in every town brewing the beverage in a variety of concoctions using beans grown in exotic places and tailored to tantalise every tastebud and palate. Nowadays there are more snobs to be found in a coffee shop than at a wine sniffing – they're the kind of people who will only drink coffee brewed from organic beans grown by Trappist monks in the mountains of Colombia.

In the meantime, tea has come to resemble the dilapidated big house outside the village where the waistcoats are threadbare, the silver is tarnished, and heedless dogs have the run of the place. In the kitchen the fragile occupants sit as close to the AGA as they can, taking tea in chipped china paid for with old money that's long gone. The cup of tea is in danger of becoming another 'relic of auld dacency',

But I reckon it is making a comeback: tea is elbowing its way up the social ladder and set to resume its rightful place as the empress of beverages. In some places even the old tealeaves are back in fashion, regarded as more environmentally friendly than teabags. A man I once knew liked his tea brewed from tealeaves and poured through a little strainer he placed on the rim of the cup. He referred to this as his contraceptive device.

Yes, tea has survived the lean times. And why shouldn't it? Among other things it has formidable friends.

I remember hearing a story about two women from west Limerick who had come to the city on their monthly shopping trip. Before catching the half-past-four bus home the pair bustled into a fancy coffee shop near the bus stop. As they sat down, arranging their shopping bags around their feet, the gentleman of the house approached.

"What can I get you, ladies?" he asked.

"We'll have tay for two and scons please," one of them replied. The man sniffed the air and said, "we don't serve that sort of thing here."

The women stood up, gathered their shopping bags, and as they prepared to leave one of them turned to their erstwhile host and said, "Mark my words, you'll serve tay yet."

There is nothing like a west Limerick woman to put you in your place.

# 38

# Measuring up and weighing down

It appears the authorities in the UK are contemplating reverting to imperial weights and measures. They are so delighted with the mayhem Brexit is causing they want to add to it by ditching the metric system. I'd imagine the Japanese and German carmakers with factories located in the increasingly reclusive kingdom will be thrilled at the prospect of more complications.

It has taken centuries to standardise measurements, and in the course of that time several common units have fallen into disuse. For instance, the 'league' as a measure of distance was used across various countries and cultures but meant different things in different places. Based on the Roman 'leuga', which was borrowed from the Celts, it originally referred to the distance a person can walk in an hour. Not a very reliable unit – I imagine the distance covered would depend very much on the height of the walker and the length of his or her legs.

Another discarded measurement is the perch, used to measure land and based on the traditional builder's pole. A perch or a pole is 5.5 yards long, 40 poles make a furlong, and eight furlongs make a mile. You'd be gone quare in the head trying to figure it all out. As for measuring land, anyone paid to work by the acre will tell you that the farmer and the contractor will have two completely different notions as to what might constitute an acre of ground.

An auctioneer friend of mine from the Laois /Offaly border recently introduced me to another unit of land measurement, the 'collop', or 'colog' in Irish. It is defined as the amount of land needed to support one family.

It was used in the west of Ireland in the 18th and early 19th centuries. Typically, a collop contained the grazing of one cow, or two yearling heifers. It could sustain six sheep or twelve goats, or six geese and a gander. A horse would require three collops.

The standardisation of measurement is a relatively modern phenomenon. It doesn't apply everywhere and certainly does not apply when it comes to some of the more important sets of life skills. I'm thinking primarily of baking bread. The current consort makes brown bread, the quality of which is surpassed only by that baked by my mother-in-law. (I'm covering all the bases.)

The recipe has come down the female line and the measurements are not so much a family secret as a matter of personal judgement. There's a pinch of this, a fistful of that, a saucer of the other and a dash of something else. I tried my hand at it but, like a ropey soprano, I was only there or thereabouts.

At home on the farm, we used units of measurement handed down by our Irish-speaking forebears. A 'beart' (bart) of hay was made up of two or three forkfuls of hay tied around by a short rope and carried on your back. Of course, 'beart' is also the Irish word for parcel. Then there was a 'gabháil' (gwall), the full of your arms of something – a gabháil of clothes from the line or a gabháil of timber blocks for the fire.

The collective noun is another peculiarity insofar as each locality has its own collective nouns for gatherings of various kinds. In our neck of the woods a herd of cows is a bane/bann of cows, I've never seen it written anywhere.

I remember once being at a famous bar and restaurant in the west. Well known for its fish it was a very busy place, particularly on fine summer Sundays. I was there with friends on such a Sunday afternoon. At the bar I ordered a round of drinks and was about to order food when the barman interrupted, "Hould on, he said, "I only take orders for drink here. You'll have to order the grub at the table, there's heaps of youngsters down there to get it for you." In fact, the collective noun he used was, 'hapes' of youngsters." I presumed he was referring to the number rather than the physique of those serving table.

On another occasion I was at a gathering of clergy and, during a break in proceedings, I found myself in the company of the bishop, a few clergymen and clergywomen. In the course of some verbal jousting the bishop asked, "What is the collective noun for a gathering of clergy?"

No one professed to know, so his lordship, with all the satisfaction of a champion jouster, answered his own question, declaring, "it's a 'whinge' of clergy."

In response one of the clergywomen asked, "And what is the collective noun for a gathering of bishops?"

"A college of bishops, perhaps?" his lordship surmised.

"No," she answered, "it's a 'dither' of bishops.

There's a name for everything.

# 39

# Global warming – it's a local thing

I lit the first fire of autumn this week. There was a nip in the air and with the gradual return to pre-Covid work habits, me and the dog are back in splendid isolation. We were feeling a bit sorry for ourselves, and the dark lifelessness of the stove didn't help.

I needed to do something about the ambiance, particularly before I got down to describing the current rural property market and its unending supply of high, dry land with good road frontage. Ambiance is vital for the making of great art. A cold house and a lonesome dog are not conducive to the flow of the creative juices. Unless, of course, I was to turn my hand to writing a country song – the forlorn canine and the chill in the atmosphere would be a perfect fit for the whine of a steel guitar.

A glowing fire would transform the house. I made my way to the shed, not only to get firewood but to retrieve all the utensils associated with the making and maintaining of a fire. The dog came along and stood guard outside the door as I poked around the chaotic innards of the out-house. Gradually I gathered the bits and pieces of fireside equipment that had been banished from the grate since the heat of the April sun made them redundant.

The poker and the tongs were in a bucket of gardening utensils, having been pressed into service in that department during the summer. The firewood container had been assigned recycling duties and was acting as a holding station for newspapers and magazines. The plastic bucket used for kippens ('kindling' if you're posh, 'cipíní' if you're a gaeilgeoir) was half full of moss-peat.

I assembled the scattered utensils and recommissioned them for winter duty by the stove. Firewood had been ordered from a fellow chorister during the summer and my brother augmented this with a massive supply of kippens. We are well provisioned. Having filled the firewood container and the bucket of kippens I returned to the house with the dog riding shotgun on proceedings.

Within minutes we had a fire dancing in the stove, bringing life and light to the house. I took a photograph and circulated it to the immediates to assure them that, even in these strange and uncertain times, the home fire is burning. The dog stretched himself out on the mat in front of the flames. It looks like he won't move again until the first rays of April sunlight tell him it is safe to go outside. I returned to the scriptorium as the hint of woodsmoke wafted around the house and a sense of hibernation filled the air.

My canine friend and I would need to be careful – there is no paradise more fragile than a fool's paradise. A glowing fire in winter might be the quintessential sign of contentment, but fire and our use of it is at the heart of rising global discontent. The very future of the planet is being determined by what we burn, how much we burn and how we burn it. We could be facing a winter of real discontent caused by the poor availability, high cost and unsustainability of the things we set fire to in order to create heat, light and movement.

There's a temptation to believe that climate change is everyone else's business except mine. What difference can little old me make? A fair question in the face of the gargantuan amounts of energy consumed by places like data centres. My use of the stuff is surely at the miniscule end of micro? Maybe it is not.

Every time we flick a switch, turn the key on the car or the tractor, light the gas or throw a few lumps of coal on the fire we are performing simple actions with long-term implications.

On the radio a few days ago an energy expert explained that the innocent electric kettle is the highest consumer of electricity in most Irish houses. The problem is not so much the boiling of it but the repeated boiling to make the one cup of tea. It's a familiar story; you put the kettle on, and while it's boiling you go to the loo. When you come back you flick the switch to boil it again, and just as it's bubbling a neighbour drives into the yard to borrow the trailer. You give him a hand to hitch up and you come back in for the third attempt to make the cup of tea. You flick the switch again and then the phone rings. By the time you eventually make the cuppa you've boiled the kettle four times.

The simple things add up to a complex problem, consciousness is key to a solution.

The fire is grand, there's great heat in the house, but me and the dog would not want to get too comfortable in our own bubble. We are part of the bigger picture.

# 40

# Too much of everything

I am beginning to look at decluttering. I haven't read much about it, but I have listened to decluttering experts on TV and radio talk about the joys and pains of the process. I must admit I take what they have to say with a grain of (organic) salt. Ultimately, they are encouraging me to add to the clutter in my house by buying yet another book.

They all agree there is great liberation in getting rid of things you no longer need, that stripping your goods and possessions down to the essentials frees up the mind and spirit. But why do we gather all these things and why are we so slow to get rid of them when they are no longer of any use?

Moving house is a great opportunity to deal with the non-essentials. It forces you to make real choices, especially when the removal van is parked at one side of the back door and the skip is sitting at the other. You ask serious questions about the wisdom of hauling uselessness from one place to another.

Farmers make great clutterers, and what they hold on to has the potential to take up acres of space. Some farmyards are so cluttered they look like a breaker's yard, an outdoor museum and a sculpture park all in one. You know the scene: a mowing bar that hasn't cut a blade of grass in 20 years sits beside a muck-spreader that last saw service when the first Gulf War was at its height. An old Nuffield tractor has briars protruding from every orifice climbing up through a cab that contains more biodiversity than a small forest. The list goes on, a manure spreader held together by rust, a single furrow plough without a sock and an exhausted square baler whose knotter caused mental anguish to two generations.

I look around me in my place of work. There are shelves of books I have read but will never reread and copies of programmes, policies and procedures that are old enough to be offensive to half the population. Finally, some books with pristine spines stand unsullied and unread and may remain so. Dare I say it, but perhaps were a lockdown of sufficient length and severity might be imposed it might afford me the time plough through them.

Meanwhile, out of doors a collection of discarded hardware needs dealing with. It includes a rusty wheelbarrow (which the current consort remodelled with the front bumper of the car), an old pink bicycle with white tyres and a menagerie of steel and other detritus left after the building of the house.

There are multiple reasons for not disposing of this stuff. Laziness and procrastination are among the main factors – if I'm not falling over it, it can stay where it is.

But then there is the attachment, there is some connection that makes you want to keep things. Every time I look at the pink bicycle, I remember our eldest child learning to cycle and how she would spend hours on end pedalling around the yard singing to herself.

There is a benign attachment to things. However, there is also the attachment that arises from insecurity, 'what if I need it some day?'

Often the desire to hold what we have is based on insecurity rather than need. Multiply this behaviour by a few hundred million and it is obvious why we in the west have too much of everything. We have run out of space for it. There was a time people rented storage space when moving house or during renovations, now some people rent it permanently. Unfortunately, we can't store all the surplus food we buy, with the result that about 30% of it goes straight from the fridge to the bin.

I remember a scene from the book, Wolf Hall, the first in a trilogy written by Hilary Mantel and based on the life and times of Thomas Cromwell. I was really struck by a passage where Cromwell was making a will. Among the most important bequests were his clothes. Each garment was itemised and bequeathed to a particular person. Clothes were extremely valuable in those days. Every item was individually made from scarce material that took a lot of labour and skill to refine and finish. Fine clothes represented hours and days of work. In our world there is little regard for time, material or labour.

Some years ago, I recall talking to a young relative of mine after she spent six weeks in Tanzania. While working in a rural school she lived with a local family. One of the things that stood out for her was the complete absence of surplus. At mealtimes there was enough for that meal, between meals there was no fridge to go to, no biscuit tin full of goodies and no bowl of fruit.

The need to declutter is not just a personal thing, it's a global problem created by a first world that's blazing an unsustainable trail of consumption.

# 41

# Waltzing to the centre of power

I have been to a number of weddings lately, wonderful events, even in the shadow of the pandemic. They were celebrated in great style and with great gusto. Weddings, in truth, are a vote of confidence in the future. Most cultures make a big deal out of the occasions, for that very reason.

Of course, there is a deeply personal side to them; the happy couple are delighted to have found one another and parents are delighted their child has found a life partner.

In the not-too-distant past, 'the going away' was a big part of the wedding celebration. Before the end of the dancing the couple retired to change out of the formal wedding gear and reappeared in their 'going-away outfits'. After 'oohing' and 'aahing' at the gorgeousness of the new clobber the guests made a human tunnel all the way from the dance floor to the carpark. The newly-weds, holding hands and bending down, tried to get through the tunnel as quickly as possible and escape the melée of poking, pulling, backslapping and hugging. Then they were off on the honeymoon in a graffiti-covered car with tin cans and all kinds of clattering things tied to the rear bumper.

Despite the madness of it, that part of the celebration was very symbolic, signifying the beginning of a new life and the first exciting steps in building a future together.

Older guests, after they had an opportunity to waltz around the floor a few times, would sit back and let 'the youngsters' at it. As soon as the 'going away' was over, they'd go away too. She'd look at him and say, 'Come on Tom, anyone could do our business here now." He'd finish the last dregs of his pint; she'd ask him for the car keys and they'd make their way home to their own kitchen.

As she exchanged the claustrophobia of new shoes for the comfort of her slippers, he'd make the tea and pop a slice or two of bread in the toaster. Then they'd sit and review the day, talking about who looked well and who was shook, who drank too much and who could do with drinking a bit more. After agreeing that the pair who got married were a grand couple, they'd made their way to the bedroom and ease themselves into the bed, content that the world as they knew it was in order.

But that was when the older generation believed they had made the world a better place, one that the youngsters could only make better. I'm afraid my contemporaries have little reason to believe they are handing a better world to their children.

Yes, in Ireland, as in much of the affluent West, the material quality of life has improved massively since the 1950s. Most indicators show an improvement in life-expectancy, average incomes, health care, employment prospects, job satisfaction and the like. The evolution of social policy has made for greater equality and inclusion.

However, the same period of time has coincided with an accelerated degradation of the planet. So much so that, if we continue as we are, we will consign our children and their children to a life on the edge of extinction.

At weddings we look on nervously, we know the revellers are not going to have it easy. In some ways these celebrations have the frenetic energy of a village dance the night before the young go off to war. It is a war we have left them with.

Some scientists describe these times as the 'Anthropocene epoch'. According to National Geographic the term describes the period of history that came about when human activity began to have an impact on carbon and methane in the earth's atmosphere. Some say it began with the Industrial Revolution in the early 1800s, others say it started after the testing and use of the first atomic bombs in 1945. Many contend it started in the 1950s during what is called the Great Acceleration, a term describing a dramatic increase in the kind of human activity that impacts the planet.

Things have accelerated so fast, only this week the Secretary General of the United Nations, António Guterres, described what is ahead as a "hellscape of temperature rises". My generation has benefitted hugely from the Great Acceleration and seems happy ignore the reality that those who come after us will pay the price.

Our politicians, who depend hugely on the 'grey vote' to get elected, believe they are doing our will when they question and nit-pick every initiative and piece of legislation that seeks to combat climate change.

We need to let them know that we are worried for our children and grandchildren. When we are done waltzing at the weddings, perhaps we should start walking to the centres of power where the many sins of emission are forgiven and the sins of omission are many.

# 42

# Stable and constant

I have often wondered where the term 'bucket list' originated. It appears to have been invented by screenwriter Justin Zackman for his 2007 film, The Bucket List, and refers to the list of things you want to do before you kick the bucket.

When put like that there's a sort of dark finality about the compiling of the inventory. I suppose nothing concentrates the mind like a deadline, particularly the ultimate deadline. On the other hand, it can free us up to do extraordinary things and fulfil dreams that the ordinariness of life has all but smothered.

One of the things I imagine doing, while I still can, is spending a few months, or a year even, catching up with friends, making meaningful contact with people with whom I have lost touch. I have a notion of turning it into a road-trip, a sort of pilgrimage, revisiting old friends and recounting the joys and sorrows that characterised the particular period of time when our lives and paths crossed. In some cases, it might be an opportunity to resolve the unresolved, or even to leave them so. I am reminded of that lovely phrase used by storyteller Eamon Kelly to park an element of a story when he'd say, "things reshted so."

Having lived different lives in different places I calculate that I have friendships stretching across ten distinct phases of my existence. In imagining a trip across the ten phases I expect there would be great craic in the reminiscence, laughing about things that were disasters when they happened. Like the night I had to board a bus full of tourists at Rome's Fiumicino Airport and inform them that, due to circumstances beyond my control, they would be spending the first five days of their visit to Rome in Anzio, a seaside town over 63km south of the city.

Anzio is a lovely place, made famous by the Allies' amphibious landing in January 1944 and the ensuing battle that lasted five months. I had to battle with a small army of disgruntled tourists for five days, launching charm offensive after charm offensive until accommodation in Rome was secured.

That memory was triggered as I sought to identify over the various phases of my life. I'm sure many more memories will be triggered if I ever get around to meeting the people I worked and played with across the decades. Some, I'm sure, will be delighted to reconnect, others may wonder where I have been for the last 30 years and why this sudden urge to meet up. But, by and large, my experiences to date in coming across old friends would suggest that friendships are rekindled and find a new depth brought on by the passage of time.

Writing this I am conscious that for many farmers their circle of friends has been stable since their school days, determined by geography, occupation and inheritance. Some are living in the house they were born in, where those before them were born, and those before them again. Others are living a stone's throw from their birthplace. Friendships formed from their earliest years in primary school and secondary school, in many cases, remain the same.

Friendships among farm families often have roots that go deeper than anyone can remember. There is a stability and a warmth to them that are not made manifest in hugs and kisses but will find expression in nods of recognition and the gentle squeeze of a hand. The richness, depth and constancy of these connections are often envied by those of us who have moved away.

Permanence is a feature of farming families and their friendships, especially for those who stay where the land is and, as the cliché goes, grow where they are planted. Impermanence, mobility and 'being moved around' was traditionally associated with occupations like the guards and bank managers. It was also associated with clergy and members of religious orders. However, in the Benedictine order there's a huge value placed on what they call 'stability', in physically staying in a certain monastery for life. It implies constancy and perseverance.

Stability, hospitality and community are among the ten core values of the Benedictine way of life, values held in common with farming communities everywhere. Sometimes those who stay at home feel deprived of the opportunities enjoyed by those who chose to stretch their wings.

Those who took to the wing often envy the stability of those who stayed, who will never need to travel the country or the world to find the people and places that made them.

# 43

# Stuck in the colonial comfort zone

The revisitation of the Treaty is fascinating, even more so than the commemoration of the Easter Rising and the War of Independence. While the latter had their subtleties, gore and glory, to most Irish people they represented a clear fight between 'them' and 'us' where 'they' were the baddies 'we' were the goodies.

When it comes to the Treaty it isn't easy to be so black and white. With 100 years of hindsight, we are prepared to acknowledge the myriad of subtleties associated with the negotiations, the signing of the document and the bitter-sweet outcomes. The 'them and us' dimensions are not as clear-cut and the fall-out continues to this day in the reality of a divided island and a constant need to perform running repairs on the frayed edges of unfinished business. Sunningdale, the Anglo-Irish Agreement, the Good Friday Agreement and even the accursed Northern Ireland Protocol come to mind.

One of the key dealmakers for the British during the Treaty negotiations was the eventual, albeit reluctant, acceptance by the Irish delegation of dominion status. This was regarded as a deal breaker by those in Ireland who opposed the Treaty. We ultimately broke free of that status when John A Costelloe's government declared the republic in 1949.

But did we really break free, or do we still carry the residue of a dominion mentality? It is interesting to note that when we compare ourselves to other countries, or when we seek to emulate the achievements of other nations, we inevitably look to English-speaking ex-colonies governed by the descendants of white Europeans. How many times will we compare ourselves to Canada, the US, Australia and New Zealand before comparing ourselves to countries closer to home, similar in size and with whom we share membership of the EU? Such countries would include the likes of Denmark, Finland and Austria.

While the common-law legal system we share with other ex-colonies makes comparison easier, the use of English as the first language seems to be the major binding agent. Despite all our protestations to the contrary we are in our comfort zone when dealing with our former colonial fellow travellers, be it the ex-coloniser or the ex-colonised, of European descent.

The working out of Brexit might convince us to look for soulmates and trade-mates in places other than the far-flung pockets of a former empire. While the UK is getting ready to launch itself as Global Britain (without the coloniser's whip) it would be a good time for us to get off the continental shelf and become truly European.

One thing we have brought with us from our days in the empire is the arrogance of the English speaker. Perhaps now we will take up the task of learning other European languages more seriously, thereby smoothing the way for deeper connections with our partners and neighbours.

People regard it as a matter of profound respect when you take the trouble to learn their language. In this regard I'm thinking of Paddy Byrne of Tullow in Co Carlow, a man who set up a hydraulic cylinder manufacturing enterprise in the 1970s. His group of companies is now a global player in that business. It captured a major segment of the market in Germany where sales mushroomed when Paddy decided to learn German. This he accomplished in his fifties and even though his formal education had finished in his early teens he wasn't afraid of the challenge.

If we look at the linguistic skills of some of our European neighbours, it will show us what is possible. The Dutch are superb when it comes to languages where some people speak four or more, particularly, Dutch, English, French, German and Spanish. They also read in those languages.

I am afraid we may not rise to the challenge, especially if we keep harping on about the fact that, after Malta, we are the only English-speaking country in the EU. While this is a useful asset it is also a pigeon-hole we could do well to avoid if we want to remain 'at the heart of Europe'. Demographics are already pushing out the boundaries for us. According to the 2016 census, 612,018 residents, or almost 13pc of people in Ireland, speak a language other than Irish or English in the home.

It is 100 years since we fought a bitter civil war over a treaty where dominion status was a key issue. One side totally opposed the notion and the other grudgingly accepted it as a delaying tactic on the road to greater freedom – what great bitterness over so narrow a gap.

Now that we are politically free of imperial imposition is it not time we ditched the mentality and the trappings as well? We would do well to shed the unspoken chauvinism around the supremacy of English and the subconscious belief that the Anglophone world is a cut above the rest.

# 44

# A time for embracing

A range of emotions and realities collide at this time of the year. Within a few short days, we find ourselves looking back and looking forward. The experience of Christmas is a mix of joy in the present and nostalgia as we look back to the "ghosts of Christmas past'. Suddenly, the focus switches to the New Year and to the future. We go from a season of plenty to a time of hard choices as the mistletoe and wine give way to sackcloth and ashes. One could say that, overnight, we swap the red nose of Rudolf for the hard nose of January.

It is interesting to note the contrasting ways we view winter before and after Christmas. In December we long for snow and frost while in January they will represent nothing but hardship. December and January represent dramatic changes that can be hard to handle.

As I write this, I have just returned from taking two of the fledglings to the bus. Their bedroom doors are ajar once again. For a short time the house was full and all the places at the table were re-occupied as if they had never been vacated. Meals became extended affairs peppered with chat about Tic-Tok, Kardashian bottoms, billionaires blasting themselves into space and why Omicron might be a just reward for the selfishness of the wealthy West.

In between meals there was constant grazing and nibbling of chocolate, jellies and exotic biscuits and an avoidance of the weighing scales. As soon as the daily supply of milk and bread was secured the car was parked and a glass or two of vino collapso could be enjoyed. Little socialising outside the house was possible since there were few places to go in these plague-ridden days.

But an end comes to all good things. The clock ticks inexorably towards the New Year and suddenly it is the time to drive the young to bus and train. Suitcases are filled and the rooms return to their default setting of suspended animation as fledgling wings get stronger and the flight trajectory gets longer.

The journey to the station passes in silence. After a few words and a hug they turn and, with the wheeled suitcase rumbling behind them, join the departing throng. You watch and realise how the reality has shifted, how the horizon you once had your eyes set on is theirs to reach for. You are now the custodian of the places and the memories that formed them, the polisher of their touchstones.

Thankfully, this shift does not happen as suddenly and violently as the jump from Christmas to New Year, it's a dawning that comes at its own pace and with its own gentleness. At the beginning there is resistance, a denial that time and tide will change anything. There's a determination to hold on and hold out, we are not ready to share the cockpit with a new generation.

Much of the language and imagery around our approach to the future verges on the avaricious. We talk about grasping opportunities, taking things by the horns, holding tough. However, the natural passage of time and the wisdom of the years seem to favour embracing what is ahead and gradually letting go of what is no longer appropriate for us.

I'm not a great one for resolutions, I tend to view them as arbitrary, elastic things that eventually lose their firmness and, like loose trousers, will only serve to embarrass you and expose you to ridicule. Rather than make resolutions for 2022, I hope to adopt a notion, or a word for myself. The notion I have in mind is that of embracing. For the next year I'm not asking myself what will I avoid, what will I confront, I am asking myself what will I embrace?

As an approach to change I reckon it is a positive way to make new things happen. It beats strapping oneself into a straitjacket of inflexible resolutions. When it comes to dealing with the passage of time, embracing the possibilities of a new reality is far healthier than brooding on what was or what might have been. It creates a place where a new generation is accommodated and encouraged,

The house is quieter now, a new rhythm is being established and the great wheel of life continues to turn as December becomes January.

# 45

## An uneasy peace

Isn't it such a woeful pity the foundation of the State and the Civil War are often found in the same sentence and named in the same breath?

Their utterance together serves as a constant reminder that what should have been our proudest moment became our most bitter memory. And it lingers.

It is as if a great family celebration is forever tainted by an unspeakable tragedy. After almost eight centuries of waiting for the Spanish, the Stuarts and the French to liberate us we had eventually done it ourselves. What an achievement that was. But the joy was sucked out of the moment and the vacuum filled with hate, death, destruction and long memories.

Have we ever gotten over it? I don't know if we have. The early years of the state, those times when the young country should have been excited about itself, a period that should have been characterised by energy, creativity and initiative, were years of numbness and a kind of suspended animation.

Ours was the first country to be colonised by Britain and, aside from America, one of the first to break free. The 1920s were exciting and turbulent times across Europe. In the wake of the Great War a plethora of new countries had emerged including Czechoslovakia and Yugoslavia while older countries like Poland and the Baltic states had re-emerged.

It was a great time to be a young country, the old empires were in terminal decline, and Ireland could have been a leading light in the emerging dispensation. Instead, we fought one another to a standstill. The upheaval, the violence, the division and the hatred that permeated communities and families for years after the civil conflict left the country collectively traumatised.

In the popular understanding of the causes of the Civil War, partition is seen as a a crucial issue. However, the nature of the state envisaged in the Treaty was the vital focus of debate and division. Dominion status with the British monarch as head of state was anathema to those committed to the establishment of a republic. Supporters of the Treaty, who regarded themselves as equally committed to the republic, were willing to accept the terms of the Treaty as a temporary arrangement on the road to full freedom. Words led to war.

When it was over, many participants on both sides could never speak of what was done to them or about what they did to others. The memory of things that happened in the heat of battle, at dawn in the execution yard, or in the damp ditch remained the triggers for nightmares until the eternal sleep erased them.

The war never finished, it ground to a halt and in its wake a form of life emerged, laden with silent recrimination, little reconciliation and no peace.

Like someone recovering from trauma, the simple business of keeping body and soul together took all our energy. Once the guns were put away both sides took refuge in the rigid certainty of the church and took cover behind the conservative middle-class preoccupations of the new government. These accommodations left us in a state of cultural and economic stasis for most of the next 50 years.

Economically the first government of the Free State was preoccupied with balancing the books. It made every effort to avoid the fulfilment of doomsayer prophecies predicting the new state would be an economic basket-case once it broke away from Britain. Aside from the Shannon Hydroelectric Scheme of the late 1920s few risks were taken and little creativity was evident in that first decade of independence.

Indeed, it should be said that the aforementioned scheme was a brave and visionary undertaking. Along with the smooth transfer of power after the 1932 election, which copper fastened the democratic nature of the state, these stand out as massive achievements on the part of the Cumann na nGael government.

Nevertheless, we all live with the unfinished business around the birth of the nation. Partition, while not a deal-breaker at the time of the Treaty, became the running sore that reminds us all is not well on this divided island we call home. This was brought to mind for me recently while watching a fascinating and lengthy interview with controversial football pundit Joe Brolly.

His life's story as a boy growing up in an activist family in staunchly nationalist Dungiven mirrors the story of the country. People might recall, a number of years ago, Brolly donated one of his kidneys to a club mate who needed a kidney transplant. During the interview, in a profoundly moving moment, he described his decision to do this as an attempt on his part to atone for the taking of human life by people who were close to him.

Joe Brolly's story is personal and political and the story of our unfinished country. A crude instrument like a border poll won't bring it to completion, even the complex and comprehensive accommodation that is the Good Friday Agreement hasn't done this.

After the Civil War we were left with a divided island, two internally divided political entities and a sense of unease about it all. The unease lingers and we need to talk about it.

# 46

# Civilising men

While I write this, a beautiful, talented, lovely and loved young woman lies dead in Tullamore. As a parent I can only imagine that the pain of her family must have the weight of eternity.

A father of daughters, I am only too aware of how vulnerable they are in a world where might may not be right, but often wields the upper hand. They are even more conscious of this and will often phone and stay on the phone while walking from one place to another, particularly in the evening or at night.

I was born into a man's world. Aside from teachers and nuns, the only women in positions of power and influence were India's Indira Gandhi, Israel's Golda Meir and, at a later stage, Maggie Thatcher. All the 'serious players' in the world were in black suits, aside from the Dalai Lama and the Pope. In the world of farming, be they in wellies or suits, at the boardroom or on the tractor, men occupied and continue to occupy the seats closest to the levers of power.

I went to an all-male boarding school, a place I remember fondly. However, in hindsight it was not good for us young males to spend seven months of each of these formative years in an all-male environment. Women and girls, almost by virtue of their absence, were viewed through the prism of extended pubescence as exotic, rare creatures to be wooed and won, or as objects of more base desires.

Then I went on to another all-male environment, a seminary, and from there into a church, where gender imbalance is no accident of history but a clear and present policy, close as makes no difference to an article of faith.

I want to be careful not to blame these institutions for my male ills, I have to take personal responsibility. All I know is I had a lot to learn when I emerged from them. My use of the word 'emerged' might lead you to believe I was locked away and sheltered from the world, but I wasn't. I was very much at the heart of life, accompanying people through the ecstasies and agonies that go with being a human on the planet. Ironically, one of the spiritual goals was to be 'in the world but not of the world'. This often found people like me floating around in a parallel universe.

I most certainly emerged as a man that needed a lot of work done. When I met my wife, I would say one of the first things she had to do was civilise me. In writing this I do not want to cast aspersions on my former colleagues – the vast majority were and are the gentlest and most lovely of men. I am talking for myself, whatever it was about me, the years in predominantly male environments left me incomplete.

Fate decided I needed to be taken in hand and it gifted me with a family of women who, I'm sad to admit, have to continue their mother's work of reformation and transformation. This occasionally means eyeballing me to explain in simple terms how the world is different for women and often not that pleasant at all.

The reality of modern men, while it is much changed from that experienced by our fathers and forefathers, still has strong residues of what went before. Millenia of misogynism and sexism do not disappear over a few decades, they are deeply embedded in the fibres of our culture. Even among men who might regard themselves as sophisticated, sane, and urbane there are strong traces of the sins of our forefathers. These find expression in the nods, winks and nudges that still go on between men when women are out of sight, out of earshot, and even when they are not. Potent traces are to be found in men's social media traffic, in our emails, in the things we receive and forward.

While these might be regarded as a bit of craic, they stir up the residue of something deeper and more sinister, something that has not gone away, you know. Once stirred up it can create the conditions for rotten things to happen.

Like every father who loves his daughters the murder of Aisling Murphy has made me face the volatile nature of the world they live in. It has also made me ask myself how I, as a man, in thought, word or deed, contribute to this volatility and to the persistence of a culture where some men conclude they have a license to kill.

# 47

# A daffodil away

The first hints of spring are lovely. Even the slightest pip and ping of birdsong raises a hopeful eyebrow. These days you can almost hear the earth stretch itself in a languorous yawn as it prepares to shake off the detritus of winter.

The almost sudden end to the pandemic took us by surprise, as if the apple blossoms suddenly bloomed and the swallows swooped low well before their time. Yes, the news that the days of social distance might soon be consigned to history gave a particular loveliness to the early signs of spring.

Of course, it is not all over. We could yet get a frost on Good Friday and snow at Easter but, for the moment, we will embrace the good of what is and rejoice in the hope of what is to come.

It will take decades for historians, social scientists and experts in many disciplines to measure the impact of these last two years on the planet and on the progress or otherwise of its dominant species.

I am reminded of the reputed response of a long-serving member of the Chinese politburo when he was asked for his opinion on the impact of the French Revolution, "It's too early to tell," he said.

Prior to any assessment, those of us lucky enough to have survived the virus need to be grateful and say 'thanks.' At the risk of resorting to cliché, the greatest sacrifice most were asked to make was to stay at home and keep out of danger. Meanwhile legions of our fellow country women and men took their lives in their hands every day they went to work.

This was particularly frightening in the early days when they faced a deadly virus about which little was known except that it was sickening and killing people in their thousands. Yet, these incredibly brave and dedicated people, our neighbours, family, colleagues and friends, continued to go to work in hospitals, care homes, GP surgeries, Garda stations, shops, factories and schools to ensure we were all fed and kept safe. They saw to it that those who needed medical care got it and those going on the last journey did so with the warm hand of another human being holding theirs.

Our political leaders and our public servants also deserve our thanks. Obviously, ever before Covid came along there was a pandemic plan in place, and we are fortunate to have political leaders with the courage and single mindedness to implement it. It has to be recognised that both the caretaker government under Leo Varadkar and the coalition under Miceál Martin threw everything at the virus and brought us through the consequent crisis in comparatively good shape. While our bank balance may not be that healthy the decisiveness of our politicians and public servants ensured we were spared even more suffering and death and saved from the kind of societal chaos that can accompany great upheavals.

For many, these days are bound to be bittersweet. I am reminded of a passage from the introduction to The Day the War Ended, a recent book by UK writer, Jacky Hyams. It tells the stories of ordinary British people in the days around the end of WWII in Europe. She captures the bittersweetness of the time, both for individuals and society, when she writes,

"For even as victory had been claimed, there was a growing, uneasy sense, that peace, in the future, would not resemble anything that anyone had once hoped for or imagined. No chance of turning the clock back to any semblance of previously held stability. Too much had been lost."

For those who lost loved ones during the pandemic there will be no going back to normal, what was normal is no longer possible. In its wake the pandemic leaves absence and void and an eternity of wondering what might have been. I'm sure there will be national and local services of commemoration where people can gather in the comfort and warmth of the crowd to publicly honour the memory of those who have died.

Individually we all know people we couldn't embrace when they needed us to, hands we couldn't shake and tears we couldn't dry. This is the time to make up for that loss, a time for tea and sympathy and the healing that comes from the softness of human touch and the balm of being socially close.

Spring is but a daffodil away. Soon the earth will sit up and face a pale but promising sun.

# 48

# Doffing the cap

The clothes we wear create a first impression that can be difficult to dispel.

Isn't it well I know it?

I have been at the butt end of quite a slagging since a headshot pic of me in a dickie-bow appeared on this page and others I'm associated with. My chosen attire has been weaponised by friend, reader and relative to poke fun at me.

Despite what appearances might suggest, I'm no fashionisto, I normally loll around in the non-descript and ill-fitting clobber of late middle age, the kind of stuff my children steal when going to the Electric Picnic. It's amazing how the dull garments of a certain vintage are transformed when sported by a young lassie sitting under a tree in Stradbally. Am I the victim of cultural appropriation, I ask myself?

Anyway, despite all our platitudes about the skin depth of beauty and the pitfalls of judging the book by the cover, we continue to make judgements about people based on their 'rig out.'

The recently announced changes in the Garda uniform generated pages of print, gigabytes of social media space and hours of commentary. Being only the third such change in a century it was bound to create a stir. The new Garda 'get-up' is a statement about the times we live in. Their all-new regulation T-shirts and polo shirts reflect the somewhat less formal and pragmatic nature of our age. I suppose the stab-vest is a reminder that we live in a more dangerous world, but then again, one hundred years ago the old RIC carried carbines.

Whatever their general reaction to the new rig out I'm sure the rank-and-file Gardai won't be sorry to be rid of the collar and tie. In fact, the tie is slowly becoming a thing of the past, having been ditched by trendy politicians and TV presenters. Millionaire businessmen seem to prefer polo necks.

The tie will most likely go the way of the hat, a required male and female fashion accessory up to the middle of the last century.

The hat industry or 'millinery' was big business for centuries and would certainly be a thing of the past entirely were it not for weddings, funerals and 'Ladies' Day' at the Galway races.

The original purpose of headgear was to protect that all important appendage, the head, from the hazards and vicissitudes of daily living. In warmer climes it keeps the sun at bay while in the colder latitudes it prevents heat escaping from the body. Apparently, we lose 30pc of our bodily heat through our heads.

The word 'millinery' is derived from the Italian city of Milan. In the 17th century its merchants travelled all over Europe and among the items in their inventories were hats and bonnets, hence the word 'milaner or 'milliner'. The word came to refer, in the main, to the makers or purveyors of women's hats. Men's hat makers were simply known as 'hatters'.

Overtime headgear became a fashion statement and a mark of distinction. By the 19th century top hats distinguished the upper class from the lower classes, who preferred flat caps, which didn't take up much space in their cramped living quarters.

As a political statement the hat was used to great effect. In Ireland in 1932, before a global audience, members of the new Fianna Fáil government wore soft hats to greet the Papal Legate prior to the opening of the Eucharistic Congress. This caused consternation among the custodians of propriety.

The hat has become part of common imagery and a metaphor peppering everyday language. For instance, a home is described as 'the place where you hang your hat'; if you want to participate in something you 'throw your hat in the ring'; by contrast, if you want to give up on a project you will 'throw your hat at it', if you want to conceal something you will 'keep it under your hat'.

Some people threaten to 'eat their hats' if their predictions about events are proved wrong. A friend of mine who is no fan of Limerick hurling has had to eat three hats in the last four years.

They say the fortunes of the woman's hat dimmed with the widespread growth of the hairdressing business and the invention of hair lacquer, a substance that can keep the most complex coif in place in all weather conditions. As regards the man's hat it is claimed that the streamlined design of the post-war motor car with its reduced headspace contributed its twilight. The car of course also provides full protection from the elements.

But all is not lost. I do note that the designers of the new Garda uniform 'tipped their hats' to tradition and left Garda headgear in place as an abiding part of the force's ensemble.

The hat as an accessory has not yet gone the way of the dodo. In fact, its conservation is being championed by a few brave heads.

Maybe I should take up the cause of preserving the dickie bow. Now there is a thought. Wouldn't that put the tin hat on it?

# 49

# Atlantic storms and rumours of war

It was the eve of the storm; everything was eerily calm. The only indications that a severe weather system was approaching were to be found in the colour-coded warnings issued by Met Eireann and broadcast on 'all platforms' every hour or so. The other portent of a looming meteorological disturbance was the behaviour of the dog. He rarely comes into my office but tonight he was parked on the carpet behind my chair, his snout flat on the ground between his paws, dozing with one eye open. He knows there's something coming, he can sniff it through his twitching nostrils and feel it in the marrow of his arthritic bones.

As I hammered away on my keyboard Storm Eunice was hammering her way up the coast. I was hoping to get this written before she caused the power to go forcing me to resort to candlelight and quill.

This time I had done little in the way of storm preparation. Despite all the dire warnings the last few storms turned out to be less severe than expected. Perhaps we are becoming immune to potentially disastrous events.

I normally fill a few pots and buckets with water so that we can make a cup of tea when the power is interrupted. The rainwater barrel provides for the loo and the small fireplace in the sitting room, which has no back-boiler, can be lit without fear of explosion and at least we will have heat in one room. Small things alleviate the hardship, which is generally short-lived.

Anyway, a few hours of deprivation won't kill us. It is amazing how quickly you learn to cope with the dark, eat what can be cooked on the gas hob, do without the phone, and talk to one another.

Between the pandemic and climate change we are more accustomed to having our lives interrupted by forces outside our control. Typhoons, hurricanes, tornadoes, floods and disease were things that happened in far way places with strange sounding names. Nowadays, more and more these kinds of phenomena, or their first cousins, are making an appearance at our door.

In the same vein we thought that war on a grand scale was confined to the black and white pages of our history books, to the days when Tsars, Kaisers and kings, or dictators with mad moustaches and funny hats, made whole countries throw themselves at one another. Depressingly, what's happening in Ukraine is like a rerun of the last century when warfare destroyed much of Europe, twice in the space of 30 years.

Wars are like the weather; those of us of a certain vintage remember many a storm, but we would all agree these latest versions are more severe and more frequent. Similarly, the war in Europe, it will be more terrible than anything that went before because weaponry is so much more deadly.

One would have to feel sorry for the Ukrainians, history has not been kind to them. Napoleon pulverised the country to get at the Russians, the Russians pulverised them to get back at Napoleon.

In the 1930s Stalin wiped out the Ukrainian peasant farmers, the Kulaks, precipitating a famine as he forced collectivisation on them. Kulaks were farmers who owned over 8ac of land and, while spread all over Russia, they were particularly strong in the fertile plains of Ukraine. Stalin blamed them for food shortages accusing them of hoarding and sought to take control of the supply of food by collectivising the land. About 30,000 Kulaks were shot and 2m deported to Siberia while another 3 million died of hunger.

In 1941 Hitler's armies arrived with their tanks and blitzkrieg. Initially they were welcomed as liberators, but the Ukrainians soon realised the devil they knew was slightly better. Once the tide of war turned, what was left of Ukraine was ravaged by the retreating Germans and the pursuing Russians.

Ukrainians lived in a state of post-traumatic stress until the collapse of the Soviet Union gave them space to breath and be themselves.

I thought of my fellow Europeans in Ukraine as I undertook my cursory preparations for the arrival of Storm Eunice. I was reminded of a story told me by a relative though marriage who hails from Alsace, on the Franco German border. His great grandparents saw the Prussians invade in 1870 claiming Alsace for Germany. His grandmother lived through the 1914-18 war, after which the region was returned to France. In 1940 she had a young family to feed when it became German again and in 1945 it rejoined France.

After the grandmother died, her family, while sorting out her affairs, found her attic packed with tinned goods. Her preparations were fastidious, she knew enough about humanity to expect a return of the madness. It is frightening to think that, once again, European mothers and grandmothers are filling attics in the face of a man-made storm.

# 50

# There are none like us

Our stories make us, even if we find they aren't all they were cracked up to be. They remain part of our psyche and can comfort us when there's no light on the horizon or can challenge us when we don't feel like getting out of the bed.

Our stories can also delude us. Many of the narratives we create around ourselves have to do with notions of exceptionalism, we attribute to ourselves traits of character that we come to believe are exceptionally present in our tribe.

As a boy, I believed that the Irish were the best and bravest fighters in the world. I remember being told that Napoleon said, "Give me an Irish soldier and a French General and I will conquer the earth." In recent years I read a biography of the famous Corsican and no such statement was recorded

Our neighbours on the next island are exceptional when it comes to vaunting their own exceptionalism. They are never done inventing narratives about their greatness, especially since Brexit. If Conservative ministers or MPs got a £1 for every time they describe something the British do as 'world-beating' they wouldn't need to take another rouble from a Russian oligarch.

In a jaw-dropping exchange in the House of Commons last week the Foreign Office Minister, James Cleverly MP claimed that Ukrainian fighters shout 'God Save the Queen' every time they fire British-made Javelin anti-tank weapons at Russian tanks. After firing one of those contraptions you'd be more inclined to save yourself rather than think about saving the Queen.

We all have our narratives and stories. Sometimes they reflect reality, sometimes they can inspire, at other times they can cause us to cringe. Often, they are just counter factual.

A narrative with great currency in the farming community is based on the belief that no-one works as hard as farmers. Everyone else has a soft job while farmers have a monopoly on hard work and carry the blisters to prove it. People who don't farm just sit in cars or in warm offices all day long. They "can close the door at five-o-clock, go home and forget about work until nine-o-clock the following morning."

Teachers are the worst of all, they only work half days, and for half the year. As for civil servants, they spend their lives avoiding work and get paid for putting things on the long finger. Even trades people and labourers have it soft – they too can clock off and throw the tools in the van at five o clock. What's worse, most of them take the weekends off.

A friend of mine recalls a conversation around the kitchen table involving his mother and her neighbours. They were discussing the increase in the number of farm women with 'office-jobs' in the town. "Ah sure," said one of them, "my niece works in a fancy office in O'Connell St and spends her day tearing up bits of paper."

Farmer exceptionalism in relation to hard work has transferred itself into an exceptionalism and a sense of entitlement when it comes to public money. There is a level of disregard among many in the farming community for people paid out of the public purse, but you dare not mention the amount of public EU money that passes through almost every farm gate in the land. According to the narrative, that is different, it is a reward for hard work. Yes, producing good food is hard and complex work but I'm not sure it merits the level of entitlement certain farmers have come to expect.

People outside the sector don't often comment, they just know farmers get money from Europe. Some would be aware that the CAP is a foundational EU policy with its genesis in one of the two foundational aims of the European project – that Europe would never go to war again and Europe would never go hungry again. To achieve the latter Europe has invested heavily in its capacity to feed its people.

Putin's war is playing havoc with the realisation of the first aim and has raised a question mark over the second. Europe urgently needs to be able to feed itself, and the farmers of Europe are being asked to respond after decades of investment by European taxpayers.

Non-farming citizens are now looking over the farm gate and asking questions. There is genuine amazement at the push-back to suggestions that farmers might make adjustments to their operations to respond to the possibility of food shortages.

A half positive response, a 'maybe' or 'we might try it' would have been sufficient. However, when they saw farmers pushing back at the suggestion that they might set aside ground to grow extra crops to feed their own stock, they were bewildered. The demand for supplementary funding from the public purse to pay for this was even more bewildering.

Europe is at war again and could be hungry again. What story will be told about our farmers when it's over?

# 51

# I'm off to find myself

In my young days I played music as part of a duo of guitars and vocals. My friend and I troubadoured our way through pubs and 'singing lounges' in and around Limerick city. Our repertoire included the Beatles' hit, "When I'm 64." My friend did most of the singing on that particular number and I have a distinct memory of listening to the lyrics as he sang and wondering what it will it be like to be 64. Well, by the time you read this I'll have found out.

After three score and four years on the planet there is a few things I know. Among them is this: moments of absolute clarity about how best to live a life are experienced by few mortals.

A lot of people make a good living telling the rest of us how to make the big breakthrough. They tell us not to wait till we win the lotto to do what we always wanted to do with our lives, but to leave behind whatever is restricting us and embrace our deeper calling, now!

Oh yes, it's a simple job to pack your bag, open the back door and shout, "Goodbye western, middle-class slavery, I'm off to Morocco to find myself." Very revolutionary and life-changing indeed, until the postman arrives at the front door with epistles demanding payment of a few sets of university fees.

Turning one's back on the world and striking out into the wilderness has a long history. Nearly every culture has its hermits, its ascetics and its respected odd balls. The monks on Skellig rock were part of a tradition with its roots in the life of St Anthony the Great, who took to the desert in Egypt to commune with his maker. Others soon followed until the desert became a patchwork of hermitages. In fact, Antony is credited with laying the foundations for the development of monasticism, a movement that had a formative impact on the cultural, religious and economic development of Europe.

Stories of people who left everything to find themselves or lose themselves are inspiring, especially on a day when nothing is going right, when the screen is blank and you're wondering what it's all about.

Of course, the practice of making sudden and extraordinary change isn't confined to the ancient mystics. One of the books that graced many a bookshelf in the late noughties and early nineties was Robin Sharma's, "The Monk Who Sold His Ferrari." The subtitle describes it as 'a spiritual fable about fulfilling your dreams and reaching your destiny.'

I am reminded of the story of a man getting off the Galway to Dublin train in Heuston Station. He met a friend on the platform with a packed haversack and all the appearance of someone going on a serious journey.

"Oh Tom," he said, "you seem to have packed the kitchen sink in that thing, where are you off to?

"I'm going down to the west for a few weeks to find myself," Tom replied.

"Well," his friend said, "You're wasting your time. I've just come back and I didn't see a sign of you down there."

The practice of going on retreats has re-emerged in secular form, where businesspeople, executives and busy people of all sorts take time off to spend a few days reflecting and recharging. This is a sanitised version of selling the Ferrari, and while it might do the participant some good, the ultimate aim, it appears to me, is to add value to the company and improve the bottom line.

I am also reminded of the story of a founder of one of these life-coaching companies who became something of a globe-trotting guru promoting radical transformation. He travelled far and wide expounding the benefits of leaving the rat-race, discovering your inner mystic and taking the first steps on the journey of inner transformation.

Like a lot of gurus, he wasn't the easiest person to live with. Accustomed as he was to telling audiences worldwide how to transform their lives, on his rare appearances back at head office he couldn't resist telling his colleagues how to transform theirs.

At a conference of these sort of companies a member of the wandering wise man's management team was complimented on the generosity of allowing their resident seat of wisdom the freedom to travel and impart his pearls far and wide.

"It keeps him out of our hair," she replied, "so he's not around the place driving us daft."

There are the days when the stress-free tomorrow seems to stay forever on the other side of the horizon. Even though you know better, you are tempted to do something radical to bring it closer, but there is always a mundanity to be overcome before you can get around to it.

The only real questions I have, as I cross the three score and four threshold are, "will she still need me, and will she still feed me?"

# 52

# An Easter gift

I haven't seen a full-length film in a long time. No matter how good or bad a movie might be I will invariably fall asleep about twenty minutes after the opening credits have rolled. This may have something to do with the fact that, in this house, we don't turn on the TV until the news at nine o clock.

Perhaps it's too late to settle down for an evening of audio-visual entertainment at that point. We should start watching these things earlier in the evening, but one of us is generally out at a meeting of some kind until after nine bells.

The current consort and our offspring have given up recommending documentaries, TV shows or movies that we could watch en-famille. No matter how high the recommendation or how excellent the production I will nod off. Sometimes my slumbering is taken as a judgement on the recommender's taste in entertainment, but there's nothing I can do about it, I will sleep through a cliff-hanger that has everybody else cowering behind the couch.

I don't have a sleeping disorder, at least I don't think I have, I tend to take an involuntary nap at the desk after lunch, but other than that I stay awake. The sensible thing to do is go to bed at about 9.30pm and get up early in the morning to watch whatever programmes I consider worth getting up early to watch. I am something of a lark and can often be at my desk with coffee in hand by 5.30am. Perhaps, this is the time of day I should use to fill the audio-visual and cultural void in my life.

But something deep in my psyche would make it difficult for me to sit on a couch and watch telly first thing in the morning. I reckon many farm-born people could identify with me in this. We are culturally conditioned to work in daylight and rest in darkness. The notion of watching television, reading a book or a newspaper in daylight hours is, at best, a waste of precious daylight, or, at worst, a manifestation of bone laziness.

People of my ilk would need a brain transplant or an intensive dose of psychotherapy before we could find the freedom to do anything but engage in 'servile work' while the sun is high in the sky. I make my crust in the newspaper business and, even at that, I find it very hard to take time to read the papers during the day. I'll read them in bits and pieces and online, between 'real jobs.'

In recent months I have been making brave efforts to read James Joyce's 'Ulysses'. It's my second attempt and it's proving quite problematic – the famous Dubliner's tome can't really be read in snippets and the psychological straitjacket of my youth won't let me put aside the hours needed to immerse myself in it.

It's amazing how simple things like giving yourself the permission to read in the middle of the day or watch a film when you know you will stay awake, can involve such cultural and sub-conscious convulsions.

I have concluded that I need to revolutionise my approach to work, leisure and the feeding of my cultural needs. Making such a revolutionary change could cost me a small fortune on life-coaching or psychotherapy, so, I have undertaken some DIY analysis of the issues. I offer the results as an Easter gift to my fellow-sufferers and those who have to put up with them.

It strikes me that we spend most of our lives gathering stuff, but we are not very good at discarding. Along the way we gather knowledge, experience, skills, relationships, love, hopes, and many other good things that go to make up a life. On the same path we gather stuff that weighs us down, like regret, unfulfilled dreams, unrequited loves, unexplored passions, un-grasped opportunities – and we hold on to them in our memory banks and subconscious.

This baggage clutters and restricts our ability to embrace opportunities that are life-giving and liberating. But, there surely comes a time for discarding and shedding, for throwing out the reams of unwritten rules and the lumps of half-absorbed, undigested expectations that clutter a life.

I find I have a grudging respect for people who are at home in their own skins, who are totally free in themselves, who, in a good way, don't give a damn. I'm thinking of people who can put a plastic bag on their heads when it is raining not caring how it looks – it keeps the rain off and that's all that matters at the point in time.

The ultimate search is the search for truth, our own truth beyond the clutter, our own deep truth where real freedom is to be found. The place where, if I may paraphrase John Denver, 'the dreams that have escaped us and the hopes that we've forgotten' will give us new life. It's a place called resurrection.

# 53

# Singing and dancing our way out of ourselves

There is great joy to be had in the world. Over two years ago, just before the plague arrived, the local musical society put on a show at the local community college hall featuring a variety of songs from the big musicals. Over three nights those of us pounding, pacing or even gracing the stage played to packed houses. Altogether, it was a tremendous outburst of joy and fun that, in hindsight, couldn't have happened at a better time. The memories kept us going when the shutters came down.

To celebrate the end of the pandemic and to give people a lift in the face of much doom and gloom we revived the show last weekend. With a few new numbers added and some fresh voices recruited the resulting performance played to full houses over three nights.

I'll leave the reviews to the experts but if audience reaction and the joy engendered in the performers are reliable indicators of an outcome, it was a howling success. It brought us all out of ourselves. Over the three nights those at both sides of the fourth wall seemed determined to squeeze as much exhilaration and passion out of the experience as they could.

For someone involved in community activity the experience was extraordinary on a number of levels. We often complain about the lack of collective engagement and how difficult it is to get people out of their comfort zone. Well, up to 100 people were engaged in this venture, between committee members, backstage crew, musicians, singers, ushers, parking attendants, people preparing the hall, applying makeup, operating the lights and sound.

Some old fogeys like myself, who have spent a lifetime disporting themselves on the amateur stage, performed side by side with teenagers who never stood on one. We helped them with the nerves and the youngsters helped us with our dancing steps. It was amazing to watch them come off stage, ecstatic at what they had achieved having found a whole new thrill to life, the thrill of live performance.

The solidarity among performers, from septuagenarians to teenagers, was wonderful to behold. The whole experience, from rehearsal to final performance was an inadvertent intergenerational project. Among the abiding memories is a picture of my eighteen-year-old helping a mate of mine finesse his lipstick.

The cast was an eclectic bunch that included farmers, factory workers, teachers, business owners, students, nurses, musicians, electricians, homemakers, jobseekers, retirees, guards, therapists, the odd (very odd) journalist and a French political scientist who kept us abreast of developments in the French presidential election.

Of course, the show didn't materialise overnight. There were weeks of rehearsals during which a most skilled and patient choreographer tried to convince some of us that our brains can send messages to our limbs, which, in turn, can be trained to respond with a certain amount of rhythmic order.

Every community has its geniuses, and our lakeside community is blessed with a musical genius who has the capacity to put the tuneful and the tuneless in touch with their inner Barbra Streisand or Colm C T Wilkinson.

Thankfully the cast had a liberal sprinkling of naturals, those born with it, whose bodies and voices, whose very eyes respond to every note, word, rhythm and cadence. They enabled the rest of us to reach levels of performance that even surprised ourselves.

Assembling and operating the gig rig with the sound and lighting made for a complex operation undertaken professionally by a local man who does this for a living.

And it wasn't all singing, dancing, lights and sound. The hall was laid out in cabaret format where the audience sat at tables and were served food and wine at the interval. After each performance the place was cleaned, all the glasses and cutlery washed and tablecloths were taken home by volunteers to be washed, ironed and made ready for the next night.

People often ask me where I get the inspiration for these columns. I often ask myself the same question, particularly on Wednesday afternoons and Thursday mornings when the pulsating cursor on the blank screen encourages or taunts me, depending on my mood.

Mercifully, the spark of an idea will emerge, either from the lush groves of life's abundance or from the cracks on its arid surface.

These last few weeks I have glimpsed life in its abundance, where the bottom line of existence is not measured in cents and euros but in joy and generosity, where 'divilment' and discipline join forces to take us out of ourselves. But they can also take us deeper into ourselves, to where boundless reservoirs of delight and abandon lie ignored and untouched in a po-faced world.

I ended last week at the launch of a bi-lingual autobiography written by a priest friend of mine. All his life this man has sought out the unexplored and believes joy is at the heart of what it is to be human. Never afraid to take on new ventures he is wont to say, "There is enough people doing sensible things."

# 54

# Looking at the past through turf-tinted glasses

The recent hullabaloo about turf has, if you will pardon the pun, generated much political heat. The defenders of a certain version of rural Ireland were out in force and seemed to relish the fight. There are some among them who enjoy nothing better than a good bout of apoplexy. Like fishermen waiting for the first sightings of the mayfly, they are forever vigilant, placards at the ready, stock phrases prepared, and red faces lit up at the first sign of an attack by 'that crowd up in Dublin'.

I have no strong cultural feelings about turf, I was brought up in a part of the country where we didn't save it or burn it. Timber and coal were the fuels of choice. My late mother didn't like the stuff, not the smell of it or the dust it created. Occasionally merchants from the west would arrive with wagonloads of their peatland product travelling house-to-house to sell it. As children, when their Commer or Thames Trader trucks appeared on the road we would be despatched to head them off at the gate before they had a chance to drive in and put my mother through the torture of a having to refuse them.

One day she was caught off guard when a turfman appeared in the yard unannounced and asking if she needed any, "Oh, no," she said, "I got a load from Stack last week."

"That's strange, now missus," says he,

"And what's strange about that?" she asked.

"Because I'm Stack, missus," he said.

Even the embarrassment of being caught telling fibs didn't cause her to change her mind. She kindly but vigorously directed a sweating and puffing Stack as he sullenly manoeuvred his peat-laden vehicle out of the yard.

My first real encounter with turf as a primary source of fuel came when the current consort and I settled into the early years of wedded bliss in the Slieve Bloom Mountains of Co Laois.

Being a midlander she was well acquainted with turf and soon found a bog where we could save our own. Initially I took to the pursuit like a visitor immersing himself in the local culture. However, the novelty rapidly wore off as the pain associated with this tedious work dulled the romance of the experience.

The physical agony of bog work was compounded by psychological damage, deep spiritual crises and chronic bouts of existential angst. It also posed a real and present danger to marital harmony. After a half an hour in the bog, not only did the bones in your vertebra feel like they were going to lock forever, the muscles on the backs of your legs felt ready to snap. Meanwhile your spirit was crushed every time you got a glimpse of the endless rows of sods undulating their way to a line on the horizon that seemed to be getting further and further away. It was like thinning turnips in the Steppes.

I took to loudly complaining about the quality of the turf and incessantly wondering whether this was the best use of our energy and effort. Herself, who was quite laden with child at the time, got fed up with my grumbling. "What do you know about turf?" she asked as she straightened herself and repositioned the child she was carrying in utero, "all the bellyaching in the world won't foot this stuff. Just bend your back, shut your mouth and get at it."

Suitably chastened and acknowledging my ignorance in all things turbary, I bent over, cocked my ample tail-end to the sun and did what I was told. If I were to give marital advice to men, this is an approach I would recommend.

In fairness, there is a lot to be said for a day on the bog. I have some very fond memories of going there alone early in the morning and listening to the raw sounds of the awakening planet. Somehow, in the fresh air of the young day the work was almost pleasant.

Indeed, people like me, who didn't grow up with bog work as part of our cultural diet, have a fairly benign view of turf and all that goes with it. On the other hand, those who were frogmarched to the lowlands to save the black stuff as children and youths carry dark memories of the experience.

Eamon Ryan and the Greens are often accused of political ineptitude; everything they propose is objectively good for human beings, for the planet and the species with whom we share it. Yet, they manage to give their policies all the attraction of a dose of cod-liver oil.

I would say that 95.9pc of people I have spoken to, especially young people, who spent summers on the bog, regard it as a torturous, backbreaking part of their lives they would rather forget. As far as they are concerned, only sadomasochists would idealise and remember it fondly.

Banning the saving of turf should guarantee the Greens a lorryload of rural seats in every election, at least until the experience is erased from the cultural memory of most country people.

# 55

# No-mow May

I have joined a movement called 'no-mow May'. It is the best thing I ever did. It involves no meetings, no commitments, no extra work – in fact it means doing nothing.

I stumbled on the phenomenon quite by accident. I was at my front gate a few weeks ago wondering if I'd cut the lawn or wait a day or two until it had dried out. A neighbour stopped and said, "I see you're doing the no-mow-May thing." I was tempted to reply "of course," pretending I knew what she was talking about, but that was the first I heard of it.

When I admitted my ignorance, she went on to explain that people around the world are opting not to cut their lawns in May. This is to allow the wildflowers, particularly dandelions, to blossom and provide nourishment for bees, butterflies, birds and all manner of living thing. At the same time a multitude insects, worms and snails would be spared the mangling inflicted by lawn mower and strimmer.

I can't say I was excited at the prospect of letting the grass go mad. We already have a wildflower garden and, while much of the site is wild, I keep a core section in controlled lawn condition. To describe it as manicured would be a stretch.

Over the years I have been an assiduous cutter of grass. One of the first things I invested in after buying the house was a ride-on mulching mower. I thought mulching would be much healthier than heaping mounds of the cut grass in one spot, but, like many of my attempts at doing the right thing, it was wrong. Apparently leaving dead grass scattered around is not great for ground-level insect life.

The notion of not cutting the lawn during the month of May made great biological sense, but I must admit I found it difficult to stop myself wheeling out the mower to put manners on the unruly grasses and weeds. I was having withdrawal symptoms. The sight of the vegetation getting thicker and taller while not being able to do anything about it was like having an itchy nose in a straitjacket.

As a man in late middle age with his powers and his prowess in decline, cutting the grass is one of the few tasks that gives a sense of purpose and accomplishment. It is a job that has a beginning, a middle and an end along with clear and measurable results. The fruits of my labours were plain to be seen as I trundled through the wilderness on my whining steed leaving neat rows of short grass in my wake.

I think lawn mowing suits men, it feeds our need for demonstrable achievement, our need for a before and an after, where the result is all-important. That's why women leave the grass control to us, they believe it will make the man feel good about himself without involving any effort on their part. One could argue that lawn mowing is a subliminal substitute for sex. There's a whole study in that, it might even merit a doctoral thesis.

Anyway, I manfully fought the temptation to crank up the lawnmower, even as the sight of uncontrolled growth became too much for my inner manicurist. I tried to wean myself off the desire to give the grass a tight shave by raising the height of the blade. However, no matter how high I lifted it, the thing beheaded the buttercups and dandelions and turned the daisies into patches of white dust.

I experienced a sort of Pauline conversion when the pulverising of the flowers affected me more deeply than the sight of unkempt vegetation. I soon found myself delighted to be spared the mowing job and bemused to realise the proper thing to do was absolutely nothing.

Now, I can wander the garden watching Mother Nature get on with what she does best without interference from the likes of me and my noisy machine. I am tempted to erect a sign over the emerging wilderness telling her to "Go for it, baby'. Somehow the current consort may veto such a move.

We are inclined to think that nature is chaotic, and regard 'taming the wild' to be among the major achievements of humans. Like the mandarins of all great empires, we like to believe that imposing order on a disordered world is our calling and our destiny.

The opposite is the case; nature has its own order and humans are the agents of chaos. It is time we rediscovered a respect for the way nature regulates the planet and let it take its course.

Thanks to no-mow-May I can leave the lawnmower in the shed for another few weeks while I enjoy the yellows, purples, whites and blues blossoming all around. The birds, bees and insects are certainly having a ball. Let's leave them at it.

# 56

# Minding God

I was talking to some clerical friends last week and was surprised to learn that non-church weddings now make up between 60 and 70pc of wedding services held in Ireland each year. My friends were not bemoaning this development, they were just stating the facts. I was amazed at the change.

Like them, I wouldn't bemoan it, in some ways I would welcome it as symptomatic of the honesty people now have regarding their relationship or non-relationship with God, the notion of a god, the church and its sacraments.

Some years ago, another man of the cloth told me how a friend of his, a young woman, called to tell him she was getting married. He immediately took out the diary presuming he would be asked to officiate, but she smiled and said, "You can reserve the day, but you won't have anything to do except turn up and enjoy yourself."

She was getting married in a civil ceremony. "You and I know," she said, "that I am a non-believer. I am not going stand on an altar with you and pretend that I am, even for an hour on my wedding day. However, I would love you to be there."

My friend was surprised but somewhat relieved. He went to the wedding and had a great day, no pressure and no pretence.

We all breathe easier when we don't feel corralled into doing things we are uneasy about. I'm sure there are many church weddings where the priest and the couple are equally ill at ease about the whole event. They all know deep down that much of what is being assumed and uttered is not reflective of reality. The essentials are sound; two people are publicly committing themselves to one another, and this is the essence of every wedding ceremony under the sun. For a lot of couples, the God-trimmings are an added extra.

The decline in religious practice is not a matter of opinion, it is a fact of life in Ireland, especially in recent decades when it has been quite precipitous. It has been very much accelerated by the pandemic – those who were hanging on by their fingertips to Sunday attendance are not going back to hang on again – It will be interesting to see if baptisms and first communions go the way of weddings.

While the numbers are of concern to church authorities, of more concern is the question who is now occupying the Christian ground? It would appear that a rigid fundamentalism across the Christian denominations is taking over this space, to such an extent that the term Christian is, often associated with bigotry, exclusion self-righteousness and a steely certainty. In some places you can add white supremacy to the mix.

Among some of the young people I converse with, anyone who calls themselves Christian is presumed by them to be a member of the religious right and part of a belief system that has little room for mystery, wonder, mercy, gentleness and scant tolerance for the vagaries of being human. Maybe this was always the way, most certainly there was a heartlessness and a cruelty born out of dogmatic certainty and self-righteousness that permeated a Catholic version of Christianity practiced in this country from Famine times to the recent past.

It can be argued that this was an aberration, but it is remarkable how, across religions, the self-righteous come to the top, the defenders of the faith are always to the forefront defending God from being affronted. If they believe in a God that is all-present and all-powerful, why does he or she need such defending and minding? I remember a mentor of mine remarking once that "God does not need to be minded by flint-faced fundamentalists; he is well able to mind himself."

Somewhere between the stridency of the righteous and the general abandonment of religious practice there is a danger that the core ideas of the world's great religions will be lost. I am most familiar with Christianity and with its extraordinary capacity to be counter cultural, to upend the accepted priorities and challenge the accepted wisdom.

Echoes of these ideas, like 'the first shall be last and the last shall be first' fly in the face of the accepted tenets of rampant capitalism. The proposition that 'whoever wants to be the greatest must be the least and the servant of all' is nuts in a world obsessed with super-wealth, executive privilege and celebrity.

It will be a profound loss if the challenging clarity of these ideas cease to permeate our consciousness as the public practice of belief declines. In a week when the newsfeed was gorging itself on the chaos at Dublin airport, we need voices to remind us that there are hungry to be fed, naked to be clothed, sick and in prison to be visited and homes to be found for families with nowhere to lay their heads.

# 57

# Finding a fitting epitaph for our times

One of the quirky pastimes I indulge in is epitaph writing. In rare moments when I have nothing better to do with my time, especially if I'm sitting in the car waiting for one of the offspring, I try to come up with a word, phrase, sentence or saying might capture someone I know.

In the highly unlikely event of having to compose one for my current consort I think it would go something like this; "I'd love a cup of tea." It's her stock answer to the question, "Can I get you anything?" I suppose it could be worse, she could be in the habit of asking for a yacht.

Composing epitaphs for GAA managers and players would be a very easy task these days. "Lookit", "Sure lookit" or "Ah sure lookit" would have to be part of any few words used to summarise their lives.

A man I once knew was a great proponent of resilience and his signature response to the common greeting 'how are you' was, "Erra, I'm keeping it pucked out." This would surely have been an appropriate epitaph for him, he used the phrase at every opportunity. He once used it when called on to say a few words at the diamond jubilee of the smallest, frailest and most delicate nun in the world, describing her as 'a great woman to keep it pucked out.' Incongruous comes to mind – the be-veiled fragile lady was not someone you could imagine with a hurley in her hand, and most certainly you could not envisage her standing forlornly in the killing zone that is a hurling goalmouth.

Humorous epitaphs are the best, there is something liberating about being given license to laugh in the face of the eternal silence. Mel Blancs, the actor who gave voice to cartoon characters like Bugs Bunny, Daffy Duck and Porky Pig had the classic cartoon sign-off, "That's all folks" engraved on his tombstone. For anyone with a hypochondriac friend or relative the epitaph of comedian Spike Milligan is an everlasting tonic, "I told you I was sick."

Our lives create our epitaphs, whether they will be written down or not there are words, phrases and sentiments that encapsulate the essence of us.

Of late I've noticed, in phone conversations and in-person, people are using patterns of speech that inadvertently capture the stresses and pressures currently permeating everything. Many modern phone calls are marked by short bursts of words and half words like "ya-ya-ya-ya-ya", "good-good-good-good-good" and "ok-ok-ok-ok-ok", like blank shots fired in five-syllable volleys they are meant to keep you at bay without hurting you.

They get the message across – 'say what you have to say and hang up'. If there is any sign of the conversation lasting beyond the essentials, phrases like, "I'm under a bit of pressure here, "I have to make a move" or "must catch up soon" will be deployed to bring matters to a conclusion.

However, I think there is another factor at play – most people I talk to are overworked – they have too much to do and too little time in which to do it.

During business hours it can take forever to get people on the phone and, even when you do, their devices bleep constantly as others try to reach them.

Being self-employed I have a range of small projects on the go all the time. I can find myself dealing with work issues at any hour of the day and night. I often rise early to put the finishing touches to a piece of work and email it before starting something new. Presuming the person it is intended for won't see it until much later I click 'send' but, more often than not, a 'ping' from the computer indicates it has been received and opened. The hybrid model of home and office work has made things even worse. Now there are no boundaries.

It appears to me that people are being asked to do more and more all the time, there is an aversion to taking on additional workers and, as a result, many are being worked to the bone. Where are the fruits of this labour going? Who is reaping the benefit of all this effort, toil and stress? Maybe, we are not supposed to think about these things.

Could I suggest an epitaph for our time – "Ok, ok, ok, ok, ok – catch up soon – bye, bye, bye, bye, bye."

# 58

# Ulysses Grant

So, Boris is gone off to spend more time with his families, he'll be a busy man by all accounts. But he won't be short of a bob, between the few pensions, the speaking circuit, the memoir and the children's allowance he should get by.

While they say that all political careers end in failure, the bank balance at the end of all these car crash careers never appears to suffer. In fact, the myriad of lucrative opportunities that open up at the end of the most celebrated or disastrous political careers must go some way towards soothing the trauma of the battered political ego.

The likes of Barack Obama, George W Bush, Tony Blair and even the disastrous David Cameron can command speaking fees that pay more per minute than the vast majority of us could earn in a year.

You don't have to have served as president or prime minister to monetise your past and secure your future. Lowly ex Junior Ministers can trade forever on their one-time exalted position and find themselves handy numbers as members of international panels, visiting delegations, expert advisory committees and consultative fora.

As long as you have a neck thick enough to wear a lanyard, a valid passport and a business card lauding your former rungs on the pecking order then someone will point you in the direction of a handy auld number. At the very least it will get you out of the house, add a magnet or two to the fridge door and might even put a few extra bob into the arse pocket.

A stint on the Co Council isn't a bad thing to have on the CV, either. It could get you a gig on a main drainage board or a prison visiting committee or an inter county cultural committee on the preservation and promotion of puss-music.

Not all political careers ended in the suspended animation of the lucrative junket circuit. I'm reminded of Ulysses S Grant, American President for two terms and the General who led the Union armies in the final year of the American Civil War. He accepted the surrender of Confederate commander, General Robert E Lee at Appomattox Court House, Virginia on April 9, 1865.

Four years later, at the tender age of 47 he was elected 18th President of the US and is credited with being an honourable and just man who focussed on reconciliation and reconstruction in the wake of the Civil War.

Life before the conflict had not been easy for Grant, whose attempts to supplement his military salary with business income led to a string of failures. He even attempted farming on 30ac of land granted him by his father-in-law, but this too was a failure.

He found his feet as a military leader and proved himself an outstanding planner and strategist. He brought these gifts to bear on the first term of his Presidency, but scandal and poor appointments dogged his second term.

After he left office in 1877, he toured the capitals of the world and was received warmly by all the great leaders of the time from Queen Victoria to Bismarck and the Japanese Emperor. However, the kind of financial misfortune that characterised his early working life was to strike again in his declining years.

He had placed all his money with an investment firm, Grant and Ward, in which his son and namesake was a partner. The whole Grant family had invested, but the other partner, Ferdinand Ward, proved to be a swindler and in 1884 the company collapsed leaving Grant and his family penniless.

To earn an income, he began to publish autobiographical pieces about his campaigns in the *Century Magazine*. Adding calamity to catastrophe he developed throat cancer and became increasingly unwell, but in order to provide for his family after his death, and at the urging of Mark Twain he undertook to write his memoirs before he died. Twain rescued him from a disastrous 10% publishing deal with *Century Magazine* and published the work awarding Grant 70pc of the proceeds.

With the ultimate deadline bearing down on him, and in torturous pain he completed the 285,000-word opus days before he died on July 27, 1885. The book, *Personal Memoirs* was published to great acclaim and its sales netted $450,000 for his family, a fortune at that time.

I doubt if Boris Johnson will have to endure what the great Ulysses S

Grant had to go through to ensure his family's comfort. However, there is an interesting contrast between their respective reflections on their careers, articulated as they left office. In his resignation speech outside 10 Downing Street Boris avoided any hint of self-criticism blaming 'the herd' for his political demise.

As he addressed Congress for the last time Grant admitted his shortcomings and was able to rest on his integrity, "Failures have been errors of judgement, not of intent."

I suppose it is unfair on Ulysses Grant to compare him with Johnson. The former died struggling to provide for his family, the latter sought out a donor to pay for a treehouse for his son.

# 59

# A canine addition

We have a new dog. It is 12 years since the incumbent canine, Max, joined the family. At that time, I swore I would never again go through the torture of house training a mutt of any kind. I had my fill of chewed shoes, ripped cushions, puddles of urine, pyramids of poo and nocturnal yelping.

Over a decade down the line, the burden of the years is telling on Max. A cross between a collie and a Lab, he has the mellow temperament and the arthritic genes of the Labrador. It's taking him longer and longer to straighten himself and he waddles rather than walks. I have tried every potion under the sun to help him, but nothing seems to work. I had long since decided that whenever he took leave of his dog's life, I would never again be a dog-owner

Anyway, a dear friend caught me at a weak moment. It was the first day of our holiday, the current consort and I were sitting outside a café on the banks of the Tagus River in Lisbon enjoying a warm breeze and a nice cold beer. Everything was well with us, the sun was shining and we had nothing to do for a week except walk around this lovely city, read our books and sit at cafes drinking coffee, the odd glass of wine and the occasional beer.

My phone beeped with a message from my friend wondering if I knew anyone who would give a good home to a collie pup. The little dog was one of a pair born on St Patrick's Day and now needed to be separated from her twin. The message came with a heart-melting picture.

I showed it to herself. "Why not?" we agreed, the girls are all at home for the summer and will help train and acclimatise her. Besides, we might need company when the nest empties completely for the first time in September.

I replied to my friend telling her we would be delighted to give the pup a happy home. She asked if I was sure, which is subtext for asking if I had consulted with the commanding officer. I assured her I had and received the nod.

The girls landed in Lisbon later that afternoon to join us for the break and, even though they are now adults, they reacted like excited children at the news that we were getting a pup.

Last week the eldest daughter and I travelled to the carpark of a landmark pub to meet the owner and effect the handover. It was a poignant moment; the owner was in tears as she handed us a bag with the pup's feeding bowl and a collection of toys. We promised to give her a good home.

On the return journey the new addition made her presence felt. We weren't gone 5km when the odour emanating from the boot of the hatchback told us the stress of the occasion had become too much for the little creature. We pulled into the nearest gap and, as I braced myself for the clean-up operation I began to wonder if the Portuguese sun had softened my brain and led me to make a rash decision. It was too late to change anything at that point - the pup was in the car and the anticipation on the home front was at fever pitch. Had I decided to give the animal back and returned empty handed I would have found myself locked in the newly purchased dog pen.

When we got home, the new arrival was greeted with great joy and an outpouring of affection that would have overwhelmed a lesser creature. She just lapped it up.

We were all wondering how the long-suffering Max might react, but he ignored her imperiously and continues to do so. She can jump on his head, nibble his ears, wiggle her way under his belly or bite his tail, and she might as well be a gnat. He isn't even bothered to growl.

Anyway, why am I going on about the latest dog in my life while the world as we know it falls apart around us?

'Céile', as the new dog has been christened, is a bounding, playful testament to the glory of youth. She has hit the house like a hurricane with an energy and excitement that are infectious. Every moment is an opportunity to play, to eat, to sniff and to chew. There isn't a blade of grass in the garden she hasn't explored or a hole in the hedge she hasn't gone into. Every crow that caws is sought out, every tractor that passes is stared at and every shoe that is found without an owner is fair game for the taking.

She is the perfect antidote to world-weariness, cynicism, disillusion, and despair.

As for managing the bodily functions, we are monitoring carefully, mopping patiently and hoping the process won't dull the joy.

# 60

# Devilish thorns

I tasted my first blackberry this week, the ubiquitous fruit of autumn and a sign the year is on the other side of the peak. Like all nature's seasonal bounties, the blackberry is more than a fruit, over the centuries it has gathered to itself lore, legend, symbol and sign.

Traditionally, it was regarded as inadvisable to eat blackberries after Michaelmas, the feast of Michael the Archangel, which falls on September 29. According to tradition, that was the day Michael hurled the angel Lucifer out of heaven after an attempted coup. When the bould Lucifer made landfall in hell he landed on a blackberry patch and turned into Satan. A bad-tempered angel at the best of times, the fall from grace and the encounter with the thorns of the blackberry had him in an apocalyptic rage. Such was his fury at the incision of thorns, he spat on the offending plant and turned its fruit to poison from that day each year until a new crop blooms the following August.

Michaelmas was the last feast of plenty before Christmas. Goose was cooked and consumed to mark this significant point in the calendar. Universities opened and our 'learned friends' swapped the Bermudas and boaters for wig and gown to begin the Michaelmas legal term.

Meanwhile, from September 29 the last of the poor blackberries became mere filling for pies. Wrapped in pastry the remaining specimens of the year were locked into the chambers of hot ovens where, to quote my late mother, the devil would be boiled out of them.

The devil's spit seems to have no impact on the modern blackberry. The local chain store sells blackberries all year round. Perfectly black, perfectly round and perfectly formed they don't have the remotest sign of the devil on them. While I'm not a purist when it comes to eating only in-season fruit and veg, it goes against my grain to buy blackberries in plastic packs when, if I wait, I can pick as many as I want from the hedge.

The availability of out-of-season produce is a wonder of the modern world, where you can get whatever you want when you want it – if you have the money and live in a 'developed' country. Indeed, one would wonder if 'out-of-season' is an anachronism in an age of total availability. When it comes to fruits and vegetables this availability comes at a price in terms of herbicides, pesticides, carbon miles and, often, low wages.

I remember, about 25 years ago, when the notion of 'carbon miles' first began to feature as a topic in common discourse. An image used to illustrate the ridiculous nature of what was happening was the image of two big trucks colliding in central France. One was travelling from the south of Spain to the Netherlands and the other was travelling from the Netherlands to the south of Spain. As a result of the collision their cargo was strewn all over the road and it was hard to distinguish between the loads, as both trucks were carrying lettuce. Perhaps the story is apocryphal but it does illustrate the point – or the pointlessness.

Part of the price we are paying for having whatever food we want whenever we want it is a loss of connection with millennia of custom and tradition associated with what we eat and its seasonality. We are consequently losing touch with the rhythm of the seasons and the rhythm of life as it is meant to be lived on our patch of the planet. This is symptomatic of a wider disconnection and symptomatic of a seriously dysfunctional relationship with the planet that sustains us.

The era of instant gratification has not been around a long time, so it won't take too much adjustment on our part to reduce our more ridiculous expectations. The era began for the western world at the end of the Second World War when the industrial muscle, scientific advances and ingenuity that had been harnessed for the purposes of war, were switched to serving a peace-time reality.

The mass production of armoured cars, tanks, guns and planes was replaced by the mass production of cars, washing machines, fridges and airliners. These same advances were applied to food production with the result that it has become as easy to get an avocado as an apple anywhere from Acapulco to Abbeyknockmoy.

We don't need to be slaves to instant gratification. Its voracious appetite has been eating us alive morally and culturally for half a century or more and is now threatening us physically. It is in our power to free ourselves from it, to rediscover the rhythms of the planet and the tastes associated with each season. It is in our power to recognise the devil in the detail of the weekly shopping list.

# 61

# Winding or way out of the súgáns of memory

We could become acclimatised to the fine weather. In recent weeks even the most staid of males found themselves a pair of shorts, a T-shirt and a baseball cap. Venerable lads, whose ankles haven't seen the light of day since the egg and spoon races of 1966, were exposing them to the elements.

These are the times that make memories, they give us the material for remembering the sunny summers, ice cream, chip vans and staying out all evening, sometimes playing until midnight. There was a time when red lemonade would have been an essential part of the hydration regime but not anymore.

There is a tendency in us to idealise 'long ago' and remember things as if all the world happened in a sun-drenched John Hinde postcard, but that only represents part of the truth. I certainly remember sunny days in the meadow when men fashioned their handkerchiefs into headgear, tying knots in the four corners to anchor the squares of cloth on their heads and save their bald patches from the blaze of the sun.

Looking back at those times from the mechanised perspective of 21$^{st}$ century farming, three things are remarkable; firstly, the fact that there would be more than one man working in a meadow, secondly, that these men would be out under the elements and, thirdly, that they all carried handkerchiefs.

Much has changed. Hardly anyone sets foot on a meadow these days, the work is done from the air-conditioned heights of a two-storey tractor. One could safely say that on the modern farm all the silage made, and the hay saved, is untouched by human hand. As regards the handkerchiefs, few, aside from Jacob Rees Mogg and Francis Brennan, carry that particular accessory.

To continue in a sartorial vein, back in the day, any male over the age of 12 appearing in a meadow in short pants would have been looked on with deep suspicion. It took a very hot day for the older men to strip from jacket to waistcoat to shirtsleeves. You knew the pressure was really on when the braces slipped from the shoulders and hung down by the thighs. A length of twine would be enlisted as a replacement to ensure the force of gravity didn't cause the shapeless trousers to slide earthward revealing the state of the long johns.

Were we happier then, was life sweeter? If it was, we didn't realise it at the time, and that's not much good. Hindsight is no cure for existential angst.

I have a sense of that world as one that was constantly straining for betterment, eager to move to another level. I can't say I felt those days in the meadow were part of a way of life that had its own inherent, unquestionable and timeless rhythm. Every year there was something different, a different pulse to the beat, it could be a newer mower that knocked the hay more efficiently or a mechanical turner that took more of the misery out of turning the damp green sward with a pitchfork.

The arrival of the square baler changed everything. It put paid to the centuries-old tradition of making 'winds' or cocks of hay. Associated skills and practices also disappeared, such as making 'sugáns' – ropes of twisted hay used to tie down the 'winds'. Then there was the practice of 'pulling the butt', which involved going around the bottom of the wind on your hands and knees pulling out a foot-deep circumference of hay so that the mound did not sit flat on the ground but appeared perched on a sort of pedestal. It helped keep the dampness from climbing.

Our farm and those of our neighbours were on the flight path to Shannon Airport and planes making their last approach would roar over our heads as if mocking our meadow-bound labour. Looking up, we longed for the glamour and excitement of the lives and lifestyles these machines represented. Our parents mightn't exactly have wanted all that for us, but they certainly wanted us to have the skills and capacity to have a shot at it.

There was nothing timeless about that life and lifestyle, there was a constant straining for the not yet, for something else around the corner.

The recent spell of hot weather put me in mind of those days and opened the photo album I carry around in my head. Among its grainy contents are snaps of yellow meadows, red David Brown tractors and men in improvised white skull caps bent over pitchforks while youngsters look up wistfully at the underbelly of a rumbling jumbo jet.

My own three are about to follow that rumble, to the world of London publishing, to the hallowed halls of our learned friends and to dreams of a life under the lights of musical theatre. They are unshackled from all the old rhythms. At their age I was in a seminary training to be an old man.

# 62

# An unhealthy disrespect

In this country our tendency to ignore rules and regulations is seen as a rather attractive national trait. It feeds into a notion of ourselves as people who love of 'a bit of devilment.' Our attitude to law and custom can range from grudging compliance to laxity and disobedience.

Not wishing to blame everything on our colonial past, it has something to do with an ingrained belief that temporal law originates in an alien authority and is to be resisted. There is a certain sneaking regard for disobeying what are seen as 'minor laws' or regulations.

I was a smoker for about 20 years. I remember being on a train and in a non-smoking carriage sometime in the late 1970s or the early 1980s. I happened to find myself sitting beside an old friend and as the conversation deepened, I forgot where I was and responded to the urge for a smoke.

Taking my cigarettes from my pocket I was about to light up when a man bellowed at me from the other end of the carriage, "Excuse me, you with the cigarette, I chose this carriage because it is non-smoking. Would you please quench that match and put the cigarette away or else move to another part of the train."

I sheepishly put the cigarette back in the packet and I never again smoked in a non-smoking area.

Also in the early 1980s, I spent the summers working in Chicago. I remember one day driving a work colleague to the local store on a quick errand. I dropped him at the door and reversed into the only empty parking spot, one reserved for people with a disability. I kept the engine running to assure all concerned that I wasn't staying. Meanwhile, a woman putting her groceries into the car next to mine took a great interest in me.

When she finished her packing, she walked up beside me and asked, "Excuse me sir, but do you have a disability?"

"No, I don't," I replied, expecting a pleasant chat.

"Well, what the f*** are you doing in that parking spot."

"I'll only be a minute. I'm waiting for my friend who just ran in for an errand."

"Errand my ass," she responded, "are you English?"

I was tempted to say 'yes' but thought it more advantageous to play the Irish card.

"I'm Irish, actually," I said

"Actually mister," she replied, "I don't give a s*** where you're from," and proceeded to berate me for my lack of consideration. As my late mother might say, if 'twas high up she got me, 'twas low down she left me.

After she drove away, I manoeuvred my car into her parking spot. When my friend returned, I was obviously looking the worse for wear, he asked if I'd seen a ghost. When I explained what had happened I got no sympathy, he told me if the police had come along I would have been fined $100 on the spot and given an endorsement on my license. I could also have been arrested, since I wasn't resident in the country. I have never parked in a disabled parking spot since, not even for a second.

A friend of mine, whose husband recently developed a disability, obtained a parking permit for their car. However, she is utterly frustrated at the number of able-bodied drivers parking in disability parking spaces. Everywhere she takes her husband, be it to the bank, the post office, the shop, even to the doctor's surgery and the hospital, she can find the disability parking spots occupied by cars with no sign of a relevant parking permit and, presumably, driven by able bodied drivers.

This means she has to drive around until she finds another space and may have to leave her husband standing in discomfort on the pavement or having to walk distances he is not able to walk. People, who describe themselves as having the best will in the world may have parked in these spaces 'just for a minute', but when a driver with a disability comes along how is he or she to know how long that 'minute' will be?

As someone who drives an electric vehicle, I have some sense of what this is like. Many is the time I pull up at a charging point on the street only to find it occupied by a fossil fuel car.

Our lingering post-colonial tendency to ignore what we regard as 'fiddly and footery' laws or regulations might feed our quasi-genetic need to be rebellious, but it has a price. That price is often paid in discomfort and pain by innocent and vulnerable people.

Every time I even consider stopping at a parking spot reserved for people with a disability the voice of the woman in Chicago echoes down the decades and her words ring in my ears, "Errand my ass."

# 63

# Surviving the news

The morning news is enough to send you back under the blankets. In fact, some mornings, as the talk show hosts list the topics they are about to address, you feel like sliding under the bed. In their attempts to inform, these bearers of bad tidings drain the life out of us ensuring we are suitably glum before we face the day.

I don't need to name the 'causas perturbationis' generating the bleak headlines. From war to energy prices, we are too familiar with them. The question is, how will we maintain our equilibrium and some vestige of sanity as we face the later months of 2022?

Perhaps I should consider writing a self-help book. Indeed, there is the makings of a series. A number of titles come to mind; '*Surviving the threat of nuclear annihilation in 10 easy steps,*' '*The gin-free guide to reading daily newspapers, "How to stay informed without become an alcoholic.* I reckon '*Talk radio without the narcotics*' would be a best-seller.

If this is the silly season for news, I dread what the busy season will be like. The reality that the world is teetering on the brink of conflagration led people, like the hapless Robert Troy, to believe they were safe from the poke of prying journalists. Who would be interested in a flat in Mullingar when a stray shell hitting the Zaporizhzhia nuclear power plant could send us all to kingdom come? But, there is always someone keeping an eye on 'the small stuff.'

I'm reminded of a story my father used to tell about a meeting in our locality around the time of the Cuban missile crisis when Armageddon was very much on the agenda. At the end of the meeting, a man who had great difficulty rising his gaze beyond the immediate issues that affected his farm asked if, by any chance, nuclear fallout would do away with the scourge of the warble fly. When he was assured that not even the persistent warble would survive a full blown, intercontinental nuclear conflict, he was somewhat consoled, "At least 'twill do some good," he acknowledged.

Perhaps the man's insularity saved him from the creeping madness affecting everyone around him. By confining himself to the things he knew and to issues he believed he could control – aside from the warble fly – he made his world a much more manageable place.

I often wonder if we know too much about things we can do nothing about. Do we waste lots of time and energy on a disparate range of issues and problems that are already inflicting enough damage besides adding our mental health to their list of casualties? The maxim that a little knowledge is a dangerous thing comes to mind.

With so much information coming at us from a plethora of angles we need to be somewhat judicious about what we read, watch and listen to.

While perusing last weekend's newspapers I came across a two-page spread exploring the succession anxiety around who will mount the royal throne in merry England when Banríon Eilís a Dó is called to the kingdom where her writ does not run. Halfway through the first paragraph I asked myself if reading this was going to do anything for me, aside from strengthening my conviction that monarchies should be consigned to Disneyland and the antics of royalty to the pages of fairy-tale collections.

For some real nourishment I turned to the books' pages and sampled written works bursting with food for the mind and soul.

And then there are the social media platforms. I am not very active on them, but I have bouts of scrolling through the posts on Twitter. While it can be addictive, I don't engage, and I tweet very little. The current consort is an energetic Tweeter and something of an expert on the inner workings of the platform with a small country of followers.

She urges calm when I get excited about tweets that relate to the subjects that exercise me. If I am tempted to get into a bun fight, she reminds me that many Twitterati have no interest in information or in winning hearts and minds, but are more interested in baiting, antagonising and doing down. It is no place for someone with a world view and high blood pressure.

About two years ago I published a book, a collection of these weekly columns. A good friend of mine got around to reading it relatively recently and went for total immersion rather than the piecemeal approach. After a while he said to his wife, "I feel like I'm living with this fella, he's with me everywhere – the living room, the kitchen in the bed, even in the loo."

It is the same story with us and news coverage – every second moment it feels like we are living in different situations all over the world, from a bunker below ground in Kyiv to a goat's cage high above the square in Killorglin.

We need to become our own editors, before our senses are so numbed we retreat under the bed and lose ourselves among the irrelevance of yesterday's shoes.

# 64

# Planting out

I suppose we are lucky. Unlike many others we can travel with her, so there is no goodbye at the airport. The journey to Shannon and the ritual of check-in, security, shopping, racing to the gate, boarding and belting up will mask the pain of the looming separation.

She is off to do what her heart, her soul and her powerful voice want her to do. But it doesn't ease the wrench from the roots and the shiver of planting out to a strange place far from the greenhouse where she was watered and warmed for the last 18 years.

The mind has been playing old movies behind my eyes for the last few weeks. I'm seeing clips from playschool when I would call to collect her and she would run at me from the other end of the playground with her arms outstretched screaming 'Daddeee', as if she hadn't seen me in a lifetime.

And that day in junior infants when she decided it was her turn to ring the bell and summon the multitudes back to class, even though the morning break had just begun. The ringing of the bell was the preserve of the big girls in 6th class.

Then there was her first experience of performance, when playing the fairy godmother in an improvisation of Cinderella she counselled the hapless Cinderella to ignore the ugly sisters telling her 'never mind those two old bas***ds'. She explained to the gobsmacked teacher that she didn't realise it was a bad word – which possibly said something about the amount of time she was spending with her profane father.

I was at home with her, trying to be a stay-at-home dad. When I wasn't at my wits' end, we would roll around the floor and she, like a little big woolly doll, rolled with me. We'd watch episodes of the Little Red Tractor and Postman Pat avoiding for as long as possible the chaos and frustration of homework. It often ended with the two of us in tears.

On these September days I remember her on my shoulders at the Electric Picnic belting out with gusto and abandon every word of the Mumford & Sons' anthems as people pointed at her from the crowd, bemused by this little powerpack whose every sense and sinew responded to each beat and cadence.

'My lovely rose of Clare' was her first song, surprising us all at her sister's confirmation party. At the height of the sing-song she snuck up beside me and whispered that she wanted to sing. Since then, she has never stopped, singing always and everywhere, delighted to use what was given to her. And not happy with just using it she worked on it, trained for it and then stole my old guitar when COVID kept us all at home. After the plague she took to standing at street corners in Limerick busking.

No great lover of the corral of academics she has always been a follower of her passions. With the hurley she did her best to master the skill and cried with frustration when she couldn't reach the heights she aspired to. The oval ball and the mad abandon of the rugby ground gave her more space to use her presence, her voice and her determination as she shouted, ran, tugged and tore, driven by a hatred of losing.

There was darkness too, when fear and feelings of friendlessness broke her heart and bruised her spirit, but the pain was not in vain as it took her deep and filled her songs with soul.

This year she filled a stage and a hall with her song, her voice and her presence. When it was over, she knew what she wanted to do with the rest of her life.

This evening, her siblings had their moments with her before they left to carry their shared memories to the Electric Picnic and celebrate our fond connection with our beloved Laois.

So, we take her and leave her in the space we hope will be the place of her resurrection. We console ourselves saying how lucky she is to be following the dreams of her heart, even if it is only for a few leagues. She's on her yellow brick road, a road not many get to stand on let alone walk along.

At home we keep our sadness to ourselves. For my own part I want my missing of her to be my own, I don't want to share it, I hold on to it because the missing of her is the having of her, the holding of her and the not letting go of her. We turn away in the bed and wind our own umbilical piece of her around our own hands.

Sometime in the night we find one another before we wake to the taking and the leaving of her to a new life, with and without us.

# 65

# Freed at last from the gilded cage

The death of Queen Elizabeth put me thinking. Like many Irish people, I break out in a rash at the notion of monarchy and my immediate reaction to her royal expiry was to ignore it or grunt about it. However, the news junkie in me wouldn't let me avert my eyes from the drama and pageantry and as I moved beyond the knee-jerk I realised that there was more to this than met the prejudicial eye. There was the woman, the history and the office.

As a human being she lived a predetermined life, one that was laid out for her from the beginning. In that regard, she had a lot in common with many Irish farmers. She was like the son chosen to be the farmer whether he wanted it or not. For anybody who is 'earmarked', or whose course of life is predetermined there comes a time when the path has to be embraced or rejected. Queen Elizabeth wholeheartedly embraced her destiny at a very young age, as articulated in a much-quoted speech she gave during a visit to South Africa.

No matter what we may think of monarchy as a concept, the path she found herself on consigned her to a life in a cage, albeit a gilded one. It was a life that could have been lived in bitter shadows if there had been a failure to fully embrace or, indeed, totally reject the destiny laid out for her. The middle way has all the attraction of a flat pint.

A lot of people can identify with Queen Elizabeth, simply on a human level. To quote Pat Shortt, when she decided to embrace her destiny as Queen of England, she had no choice but to 'knuckle down' and do it. And that's what she did.

I'm sure there were many days she looked out the big windows of Buckingham Palace and fantasised about an ordinary life. She possibly longed to do what everyone else does – go to work, come home, go for a walk, take a bus, or simply go to a film – without being preceded by flashing blue lights, a blare of sirens cameras and endless lines of people bowing and nodding.

I'm not sure if the lavish material benefits that come with being a royal personage could ever make up for the personal costs. At a human level the Irish people had a lot of admiration and, indeed, sympathy for the Queen.

Given our history, it is difficult for us to fathom the connection British people have with the crown. As a nation whose national identity is intrinsically tied to our being a republic, we can't understand why anyone would want to live under such an outdated a historically discredited form of government. Admittedly the constitutional monarchy is far more benign that what preceded it, but it still symbolizes a history of entitlement and embodies a hierarchical stratification of human beings that has no basis in biological or sociological fact.

As far as most Irish people are concerned the Crown symbolises domination, the absence of self-determination and the political and military forces that, down through history, acted against our better interests. From the Norman invasion to the Treaty of Limerick our experience of English monarchs with executive power was one of oppression, suppression aggrandisement and treachery. In most accounts of the decades that led to independence the armed elements of British authority were collectively referred to as the 'Crown' forces.

While the sweep of British and English royal history makes for tough reading the office of the modern UK monarch is undoubtedly a force for good in how it projects itself and in the way it is understood.

Most British people believe the monarchy symbolises what is best about them. It appears to carry the soul of the nation in a mix of nostalgia, celebrity and fairy tale. It is trusted as the custodian of the interests of the nation in a way elected politicians are not. Ironically, the weekly meeting between the monarch and the prime minister is viewed by many as the government of the day accounting to the people for the way it is managing their affairs.

History will be deservedly kind to Elizabeth II, who successfully portrayed the monarchy as a benign institution. I'm not too sure Charles has the capacity to continue this. Nevertheless, whoever wears the crown will not be able to shake off the fact that the very existence of monarchy underpins the institutionalisation and the even the deification of inequality.

Royalists and royalty are custodians of a dispensation where it is accepted that some human beings are superior to others.

# 66

## If tomorrow never comes

Life is very busy at the moment. My head and my diary haven't room for much, but, in the last week, friends have found their way to me through the busy-ness and it was really good to be grounded by them and taken out of myself.

Unannounced I got a gift of tickets to the Garth Brooks concert from a pal with Longford connections – I share a mortgage with a daughter of that oft-forgotten midland county. Although the world and its proverbial mother knew Garth of the ten-gallon hat was coming to Croker it hadn't crossed my mind to saddle up and head on out to see him do his stuff.

The daughter of Longford wasn't available to travel. Thanks to a prior engagement in the cause of high art she had no time for hanging out with friends in low places. I phoned an old comrade who had campaigned with me musically and spiritually for many years and he jumped at the idea of a day out.

As we travelled northeast we reminisced about our days behind the microphone and recalled the characters we met along the way.

"Is he alive or dead?"

"I don't know, but if he's dead it wasn't hard work that killed him." We talked about blessings, backaches, ballads and bunions until we found ourselves at a park-and-ride Luas station on the western reaches of the capital.

We had to register online to pay for the carpark. After about 20 minutes of swiping, pressing phone screens and getting locked out of apps and bank accounts my travelling companion eventually managed to get himself registered to park. Alas, his bank card wouldn't work but mine did, and now it's forever associated with his parking app. "Ha ha, O'Brien," he said, "I'll be parking at your expense for the rest of my days." Being from West Limerick I wouldn't put it past him.

Other people of our vintage and socio-economic profile approached us to know how they might pay for parking, so we shared our confusion with them. If we had brought a high-vis-jacket or two we would have made a mint as parking attendants.

We got on a tram into the city centre and joined the throngs making the All-Ireland journey to the iconic stadium. The attendance was drawn from the heart of rural middle class Ireland, the kind of people that this week will have swapped their cowboy hats for the wellies as they head for the Ploughing.

Arriving at Croker, we discovered our tickets were top drawer material and were directed by the walkie-talkie brigade to the front door. Before we went in, we stopped to buy burgers and chips and paid the price of a small bullock for them.

Once inside we made our way to the bar for a well-needed drink before we settled into our bird's eye seats. We hadn't long to wait until the stage burst into life and the richest cowboy in Dublin took to the stage.

A mighty night was had by all, especially by Mr Brooks himself who was as excited as a child in a lollipop shop to be singing for and with his ecstatic Irish fans. While there mightn't have been many lollipops around there was plenty of lolly flowing in his direction.

It was a fascinating experience, especially for people watchers and the eavesdropper. Maeve Binchy would have had a field evening-and the makings of at least one bestseller. The boots, the hats, the neck – scarves, the bandanas and the cowboy swagger reminded me of the day I spent with my Uncle Denis at the Elkhart County Fair in Indiana in 1978. Irish country people can transmogrify into their American counterparts with uncanny ease.

At one stage, during a frenzied bluegrass fiddle tune when the whole stadium felt like it had turned into a gigantic rodeo, my friend turned to me and said, "All we need now is a few guys to pull their six-guns, start shooting in the air and shouting, 'Yee haw.' We weren't a thousand miles from that possibility.

The most interesting part of the night was the Luas journey back to the park-and-ride, watching well-fed, middle class rural Ireland in hat and blue jeans rub shoulders in confined quarters with edgy Dubliners struggling to keep it together. As the tram rocked its way through the sprawling housing estates of west Dublin the townies and their country cousins eyed one another with a mix of fear and curiosity. It struck me that any real talk of a united Ireland will have to address a lot more than the North-South dimension.

We had loads to talk about and lots to reflect on as we travelled southwest to take off our boots and go back to our roots.

# 67

# The heresy of frugality

I did something unusual last week, I filled the car with diesel, up to the top. I had just been paid for my latest scribblings and said to myself, 'to hell with it, I'll go mad and fill the car.' When the tank refused to take anymore, I put the nozzle back where I got it and made to go inside the shop and pay for the precious liquid.

I live in a relatively crime-free locality where the lightest of light-touch security measures are required. I often don't bother taking the keys out of the car when I'm out shopping. So, after refuelling, I was halfway across the forecourt with my debit car in hand when I thought better of leaving my venerable vehicle abandoned and vulnerable and went back for the keys. The full tank had probably doubled its value.

I went into the shop, and seeing that I treated the car to a feed of diesel, I decided to treat myself to a Cadbury's Twirl, my guilty pleasure of choice. I presented the debit card to pay my debts and the thing nearly melted with the fright.

You would think that after such an investment the machine might behave itself, but two days later it repaid my generosity by losing a portion of its exhaust.

Anyway, I tell that tale simply as an illustration of the subtle changes taking place all round us as we become more accustomed to living in leaner times. A lot of the things we were accustomed to doing without thinking now have to be thought about and thought through.

Becoming acclimatised to this new dispensation is made easier for the current consort and I as we adjust our habits and expectations to the reality of the empty nest. The shopping trolley has been replaced by a shopping basket loosely filled with half-sizes of everything – a half sliced pan, a half-pound of butter, a half-litre of milk and boringly sad digestive biscuits.

It is easier to manage change and institute a new regime in the context of this new reality. We don't have to nag people about turning off lights, turning down the thermostat or closing doors and windows. We only have one another to nag, and after 25 years of nuptial entanglement we are well capable of doing that.

Moving from the domestic to the global I think we are in for a period of national and international nagging as we try to come to terms with the end of the era of unfettered consumption. From now on more thought will have to be put into everything we do. Drop-of-the-hat decisions and purchases will become things of the past as we become aware that, in the round, it is not cheaper to fly to Marbella for the weekend than to take the bus and spend the weekend in Miltown Malbay.

The consumptive philosophy that tells us 'If it's available get it and if you get it flaunt it' belongs to a time of profligacy that is fading into the history books.

I sometimes listen to music as I scribble. I don't do it all the time, it can disturb my train of thought, insofar as I think and my thoughts follow a pattern. Anyway, when I choose to fill the ambience with sound I like to listen to Gregorian chant. Its ethereal and ancient sound takes me to a different place and I like to think it pierces the veil between here and the beyond. From the sombre rumble of De Profundis to the angelic Gloria in Excelsis it reaches into the depths of who we are and stretches to the heights of what we can be.

It is beautiful because it is simple, it is rich because it is sparse, it's capacity to take you to the edge of unknowing is grounded in a belief that it knows. It is a sublime example of less being more.

After a century of unbridled consumption, we are headed into a period of unknowing, moving towards a time when the lights might not come on every time the switch is flicked, when necessity will become the mother of frugality.

Frugality is the enemy of the economic model that has been our god since the Industrial Revolution. Simpler lives will mean we want less, we will buy less and less will need to be produced. This is heresy and blasphemy in a world where the shopping mall is the new cathedral.

The simple strains of Gregorian chant might be the appropriate soundtrack to the return of the wicker shopping basket and smaller portions.

# 68

# A random act of friendship

I was on a call when the doorbell rang and went out to answer it with the phone in my ear. I forgot to close the kitchen door and suddenly the new pup passed me out, eager to meet the visitor, was a courier carrying a substantial parcel. I could see by the look on his face that he not at all keen to meet the energetic hound pogo-jumping in the porch.

I finished the call, quarantined the dog and returned to the front door to accept my parcel. Back in the kitchen I opened it to find a fine selection of West Cork food and fish products sent all the way from Union Hall by a friend who normally sends me a gift of this kind at Christmastime.

When I phoned to thank him, he said, "I read the column about your daughter leaving for England and thought you might be a bit down. I was talking to my missus about it and said I'd send you something to cheer you up, so, enjoy it."

I must say, the present gave me a huge lift, to quote my mother-in-law, I was feeling a bit 'drim and drew'. The current consort couldn't make up her mind whether I needed TLC or a kick in the behind. She administered neither, she was too busy to be putting up with my humours.

However, she was bursting to know what was in the parcel, but, like a bould child, I wouldn't tell her. I eventually had to put the contents into the fridge and when she discovered the trove of pescatarian delights she asked, "Where did all this come from?"

"My friend in West Cork, who values and appreciates me," says I, sticking my nose in the air with all the self-satisfaction I could muster.

"You won't eat it all yourself, will you?" she asked.

"I suppose not," says I, "I'll need help."

In fairness she didn't take advantage of the open goal that response presented, and we shared many a pleasant repast over the next week and more, thanks to the thoughtfulness of my seaside pal.

The random act of friendship reminded me that so much of what we do is transactional and much of our accepted wisdom is infused with the language transaction. It is difficult sometimes to identify graciousness. Phrases like, "you get nothing for nothing in this world", "everything has its price" and even the notion that all backscratching is mutual indicate that we are coming to the point where we don't expect acts of pure generosity.

Perhaps this has something to do with the level of foreboding we are experiencing as we face a winter in the shadow of Putin and in the absence of his gas. There isn't a great sense of confidence that we'll 'get through this together'. There is a fear that we will freeze separately, in our own poorly insulated bothárns.

All across the world people looking to their governments looking to see what they are going to do. In this country our government isn't disabusing us of the expectation that they will do something, or indeed, everything. Since the crash of 2008 through to the recent pandemic, government action has been central in responding to these very different crises. The capacity of the exchequer to leverage and distribute resources has been vital.

I don't think this is a bad thing, on the contrary, it proves that the collective power of a democratic state is a great context in which to live. On the downside, it can have a debilitating effect on our willingness and our capacity to do things for ourselves.

When we think about energy we seem to think globally and imagine that the local is powerless in the face of the issue, but I think communities and local collective responses have a key role to play in dealing with the energy crisis. We could take the motto of sustainable living and apply it to energy policy – observe globally but think and act locally.

Most experts agree that the future of energy production is in renewables and the primary source of energy will be electricity. Even in the event of hydrogen becoming a mainstream source of power, huge amounts of electricity will be needed to produce the required amounts of hydrogen. More manageable volumes of electricity can be produced in every locality. There are good examples around the country of community energy initiatives using solar, wind, water and anaerobic digestion. Energy collectives modelled on the group water schemes are emerging.

Our capacity for reaching out and our need of friendship can model a way to get through what we are told is ahead of us. Local creativity and local collective action could begin to cure our helplessness in the face of the global challenges and could generate local solutions with global application.

It's amazing what inspiration can follow when a downcast husband, married to a pragmatic woman, encounters a random act of friendship. Imagine what could happen when collective acts of friendship are harnessed for the good of all.

# 69

# Our hearts are in Creeslough

Our hearts have been in Creeslough for a week or more. We are them and they are us in our common fragility, in our bone china lives – beautiful and exquisite but closer than we like to think to being smithereened into a thousand pieces.

The girl who went in for ice-cream was the daughter of all of us; our sister and our nephew stood in the queue at the post office; it was our wife behind the till; it was our brother at the ATM. We know them all, we are them all. What happened in Creeslough brought us to the edge of what it is to have a life that can be lost in an instant. How people responded afterwards afforded us the opportunity to experience the profundity of what it means to be truly human.

It was hard to keep away from Creeslough – it didn't happen somewhere else, it happened down the road in a petrol station. It wasn't done by a monster, nor was it the end result of a button pressed by the agent of a despot on another continent, it was no act of aggression or revenge. In fact, it wasn't an act at all, it just happened.

There is no one to shake our fists at to protest at the caprice of this, at the absurdity of it. There is no one to write to, no one to shout at, no one to haul over the coals, no-one whose job needs to be put on the line to account for it. We are just left on our knees on the ground hammering the earth with our bare hands at the random nature of what happened.

There is no one to blame. Even after the inquiries and the coroner's reports there will be no 'why' there will only be 'what' happened. In some ways that might make the pain easier to bear and the wounds will not be salted by bitterness.

We were all in Creeslough. We go there every day when we walk out the door, climb on a tractor, turn the key in the car, wheel the bike on to the road. While the world has more than enough people doing bad things, or careless people doing careless things, every day awful things just happen for no reason at all.

But in the sweepings after these catastrophes there are always crumbs of consolation to be found, the broken glass contains glimmers of resurrection and in the debris, footholds emerge on which we can take the first steps towards healing.

A friend of mine whose child died tragically describes herself as having had two lives: one before her child died and one after. They are different, but there is life at both sides of the awful event. What is important is the creation of a bridge between the two and that bridge is formed by arms and shoulders, tears and hugs, teapots and tea leaves, sandwiches, buns and lots of time.

In the community that is Creeslough we saw a carbon copy of every rural community in the country, where everything from JCBs to cappuccinos emerged as if by magic. The elements that hold things together – the schools, the clubs, the churches, the community councils, the hall committees all swung into action and faced inexplicable horror with kindness, bottomless generosity and a love that wears its warmth lightly beneath the practical cloth of getting things done.

We all know the people who do these things. Those that can always be depended on to be at the heart of collective action whenever that is needed, people who have the contacts and the phone numbers to get things moving.

But there is also the man who doesn't go out much and isn't one for hugs and kisses, who will stand all night in the rain in a high-vis jacket directing people into parking places. He might mutter something about it being bad auld weather and a sad auld thing that happened, but otherwise he keeps his counsel and does his loving his own way.

The teenager whose heart is broken will join the melee where cups and plates are being washed, where there is plenty of steam and water to hide the tears. There is a space for everyone, and everyone finds a place.

The mountains of food and the gallons of tea keep coming and there are people to make it, bake it and clean up. All the time, a bridge of kindness and care is taking shape to link the life that was with the life that is emerging.

For now, the loss and the forever of the pain will be softened and soothed by the caress of loved ones, the affection of friends, the embrace of neighbours and the kindness of strangers.

There is no why, there is no reason, but we are all in Creeslough, mesmerised at the incredible beauty and the absolute fragility of this thing we call life.

# Acknowledgements

The columns featured in this book appeared in the *Farming Independent* between 2020 and 2022, and I want to thank the management at the *Irish Independent* for the kind permission to publish them in collected form.

A sincere thanks to Margaret Donnelly, my editor at the *Farming Independent* for affording me the opportunity to think aloud among the pages of the weekly supplement. In particular, I want to thank sub-editor, Sam Wheeler, one of the most encouraging and enabling people I know. His eagle eye keeps my copy clean, and his wicked sense of humour stops me from taking myself too seriously.

A special word of thanks to my wife (and current consort), Louise Donlon, for project managing her most disorganised husband to walk the earth. I also want to acknowledge the love of my three daughters, Ellen, Katie and Maeve who don't read what I write, giving me the freedom to write about them.

I want to thank Dominic Taylor and Limerick Writers' Centre for the enthusiastic support in preparing and publishing the book and for the opportunity to shop local.

Finally, I want to thank the readers of the *Farming Independent* for taking the time to read the columns. A special word of thanks to those who make contact to reassure me I'm not wasting my sweetness on the desert air.

## ABOUT THE LIMERICK WRITERS' CENTRE

The Limerick Writers' Centre, now based at The Umbrella Project, 78 O'Connell Street in Limerick City, is a non-profit organisation established in 2008 and is one of the most active literary organisations in the country. We endeavour to bring ideas about books, literature and writing to as wide an audience as possible, and especially to people who do not feel comfortable in the more traditional arts/literature venues and settings.

At the Centre we share a belief that writing and publishing should be made both available and accessible to all; we encourage everyone to engage actively with the city's literary community. We actively encourage all writers and aspiring writers, including those who write for pleasure, for poetic expression, for healing, for personal growth, for insight or just to inform.

 Over the years, we have produced a broad range of writing, including poetry, history, memoir and general prose. Through our readings, workshops and writer groups, our aim is to spread a consciousness of literature. Through public performances we bring together groups of people who value literature, and we provide them with a space for expression.

We are, importantly, also dedicated to publishing short run, high quality produced titles that are accessible to readers. At our monthly public reading the 'On the Nail' Literary Gathering, we provide an opportunity for those writers to read their work in public and get valuable feedback.

The centre can be contacted through its website:
www.limerickwriterscentre.com